GOD'S CURE TO THE CORONAVIRUS

Chief Ambassador Dr. Vernard Johnson

GOD'S CURE TO THE CORONAVIRUS
Copyright © 2021 by Chief Ambassador Dr. Vernard Johnson

Library of Congress Control Number: 2021909662
ISBN-13: Paperback: 978-1-64749-460-5

All rights reserved. No part of this publication may be reproduced, distributed, or transmitted in any form or by any means, including photocopying, recording, or other electronic or mechanical methods, without the prior written permission of the publisher or author, except in the case of brief quotations embodied in critical reviews and certain other noncommercial uses permitted by copyright law.

Although every precaution has been taken to verify the accuracy of the information contained herein, the author and publisher assume no responsibility for any errors or omissions.No liability is assumed for damages that may result from the use of information contained within.

Printed in the United States of America

GoToPublish LLC
1-888-337-1724
www.gotopublish.com
info@gotopublish.com

BOOK
THE CURE TO THE CORONAVIRUS
By Dr. Vernard Johnson
913 406 4845

Table Of Content

Chapter	Page
Preface...	3
1. Cut The Chase...	5
2. Mr. President, GOD Is Waiting On You..................	15
3. History Gives Us Examples.....................................	16
4. Don't Faint...	17
5. Worship Positions...	23
6. The Life Is In The Blood.......................................	26
7. Thank God For Your Signs....................................	35
8. Excellence Without The Anointing.......................	39
9. Cry Foul...	43
10. An Uncommon Church..	48
11. How To Get Astonishing Things...........................	54
12. Much Obliged...	56
13. You Cannot Die On God's Assignment.................	61
14. A Huge Blessing Is On The Way To Your House.....	69
15. Iron Sharpens Iron...	72
16. Speak To Your Sinews...	75
17. Don't Allow The Enemy To Wear You Out.............	80
18. Turn It Over To Jesus..	85
19. Go Through To Get To..	88
20. I Agree..	92
21. I'm Declaring Ground 'O'.....................................	95
22. Step Down To Step Up..	97
23. God Is Fixing Things Just For You.......................	104
24. A Breakthrough Is Coming...................................	110
25. Continuous Praise...	113
26. Glorifying God...	123

27. Shake Off The Beast.. 124
28. Shout In Your Living Room................................... 125
29. You Do It First... 126
30. Sing In The Midst Of Your Storm.......................... 127
31. Is There Anything Too Hard For God..................... 132
32. Binding & Loosing... 134
33. Forgiveness.. 138
    Helps... 145

Major Prophet Dr. Vernard Johnson
Prayer Line. Linked with 200 Countries, territories & states combined
With the help of Face Book, Twitter, Instagram, Lineline, numerous radio stations according to the network we have 1.9 Billion listerners.

PREFACE

This is not the first time the earth has experienced a pandemic. History records that we have had at least five pandemics. Some pandemics have sometimes destroyed the entire world. Those who lived through them have left a record of why they came into the world and how the pandemics left (see the chapter on History Gives Us Examples).

This book is not a health cure attempt, nor is it a scientific attempt to cure the coronavirus, because I do not believe that this is completely a health or a scientific problem. I believe that this is more so a spiritual problem. I believe that GOD allowed this pandemic, this coronavirus to come into our world to get the world's attention. Please listen to me and allow me to develop this premise.

Man didn't create this world. (Genesis 1:1 KJV) proclaims, "In the beginning God created the heaven and the earth." Collosians1:16 (KJV) tells us, "For by him were all things created, that are in heaven, and that are in earth, visible and invisible, whether they be thrones, or dominions, or principalities, or powers: all things were created by him, and for him (meaning GOD):"

The earth was here when man woke up in it. The only book that someone has written and claimed authorship to something, and man denied his authorship is the Bible. God said He made the earth, but man denies it and says that evolution created it. I believe that God created the world and man has left Him out of everything.

What is the point. The point is, how would you like to make something and expect it to be like you created it, but it slowly evolved into something else. I think you would do like God, destroy it and start all over again. This is what God has done on some occasions. God created the world for His glory, not for the world's pleasure, and whenever He has seen that the world has forgotten it's creator and allowed sin to run rampant in the world, God has repented that He made it and many times completely destroyed cities and even the entire world (again see the history chapter).

This world is now to the point that man has forgotten about God and it has made sports figures, movie stars, singers and talented people to be like gods. Throughout history, God has allowed whole nations to be destroyed for this reason. Exodus 20:3 in the Good Book declares, "Thou shalt have no other gods before me." The government makes laws and they expect the people to obey them....God has laws and He expects the government and all the people to obey His laws too. God loves us, but when we go too far breaking His laws, He will allow pandemics to happen to get our attention.

4.

I believe God is using the Coronavirus to get the attention of the world, not just The United States! I have heard people say that we have never dealt with this sort of thing before, but after studying history, I beg to disagree. In fact, the Word of God records at lease 5 pandemics that have occurred throughout history. For further information on that, please read the chapter in this book titled "History Gives Us Examples".

God's judgment is upon the world. In fact, I know many of us have had numerous loved ones and friends affected by this coronavirus, and close loved ones have died from this virus. God is getting the attention of the world and bringing people together. We can no longer forget about GOD. We can no longer make other gods and expect GOD to keep silent. God's judgment is upon the world because of sin. If all of us would be honest with ourselves, all of us should be dead right now. 1John 1:8....and this is talking to believers (to Christians) when it says "If we say that we have no sin, we deceive ourselves, and the truth is not in us." 1 John 1:10 (KJV) "If we say that we have not sinned, we make him a liar, and his word is not in us"; but 1 John 1:9 (KJV) tells us, "If we confess our sins, He is faithful and just to forgive us our sins, and to cleanse us from all unrighteousness."

In the History chapter that I just mentioned, you will see that all of these pandemics occurred because of 'sin'.....all of them. This is what causes God to send judgment upon a nation.....and let us stop trying to placate what is happening. I know this pill is hard tto swallow, but It is difficult for one to find a cure for something until he faces the truth. We must face the truth that this coronavirus goes beyond man's comprehension, and we must start seeking GOD.

Man did not make the coronavirus.......God made it. I repeat that.......GOD made every thing.....and I am soooooooo glad that God made everything.....not only the good, but also the evil...... because, if God had *not* made evil, then evil forces (the devil) would have tried to make evil.....and if the devil had made evil, he would have killed everybody trying to do good with this Coronavirus....not just thousands. I know some of you lost your mama, your daddy, your sister, your brother, or your close friend, but if God were not in control, it would have been much, much worse than it is right now. So thank God!!! We are the blessed ones.

So this book does not offer a health or scientific cure for the Coronavirus. It is simply a spiritual approach to help the whole world get back on track to God. Before I give you what I believe is the cure, I want to cut the chase and give you an immediate Band-Aid to the Coronavirus? Are you ready? Here it is. TAKE HOT BATHS WITH EPSON SALT AND PLENTY OF SOAP IN IT. Just think about this and see if it makes sense. If the President, with all of the brilliant doctors and brilliant scientist can recommend to

5.

the world that washing our hands often for 20 seconds with soap and hot water will kill the Coronas Virus on our hands, then what will taking a hot bath in the tub....covering your entire body with soap and hot water for 20 minutes and with Epson Salt.........what will that do for you??????

Furthermore, allow me to give you another example of what heat will do. If a person has cancer, the doctor will usually recommend chemotherapy treatments..........What are chemotherapy treatments .....focused radiation (or heat) on the cancerous spot. A hot bath is focused heat all over ones body....not just in one spot, but in every spot. Again, as a Band-Aid to the Coranavirus, I recommend taking hot boths with Epson salt and a lot of soap. Please allow me to help you, but check with your doctor before proceeding:

> I'm not trying to get personal with you, but let me help you with some instructions. You cannot get into hot water....it is too shocking to the body....so draw a tub 2/3 full of warm water...make it as warm as you can stand it before you get into the tub. After you get into the tub, cut a small stream of hot water on and allow it to heat up the water.....occasionally stirring the water to even out the heat in the tub. It should be hot after around 10 to 15 minutes. Slump down into the tub covering your entire body and even up to your throat. It is said that the coronavirus gets into the body trough the throat.
>
> Then, stay in the tub as long as you possibly can. I recommend at least 20 minutes....stirring the water occasionally. If you can, take your hand and close your nose and mouth, then dip your head under the water for around 20 seconds. I know how well this will work with women because of their hair) but if you are having headaches, the hot water may also help that too.
>
> After the hot bath, drink plenty of water. You don't want to dehydrate yourself. Also, do not go outside. Your pours will be open. Perhaps, cover yourself, and put a towel on the floor and lay on the floor for a while resting your body. You should feel great!
>
> **Side affects:** this will make you look younger and more refreshed, and you will also lose some weight.....perhaps 3 to 5 pounds...depending on how long you stay in the hot water. Also, this will detoxify your body and relax your mussels. Until your body becomes accustomed to this, realize that this may make you weak; so Drink plenty of water after you get out of the tub. Otherwise enjoy your hot bath.

GOD'S CURE TO THE CORONAVIRUS   Chief Ambassador Dr. Vernard Johnson

CHAPTER I.
CUT THE CHASE

*Please read the Preface before you begin reading the chapters. When most people write a book, they usually wait until the last chapter or near the end of the book to reveal the answer to a problem, probably to keep people reading the book. However, I want to cut the chase. I am going to reveal the cure to the Coronavirus right now. I remind you that some are saying that the Coronavirus is only a health problem, but I beg to disagree. If it were only a health problem the smartest doctors and scientist would have figured out a cure weeks ago, but it is not just a health problem. The Coronavirus is more than that. It is a sin problem. The cure is found in 2 Chronicles 7:14:

> "If my people, which are called by my name, shall humble themselves, and pray, and seek my face, and turn from their wicked ways; then will I hear from heaven, and will forgive their sin, and will heal their land."

This COVID- 19 virus has been declared an 'invisible enemy' of the people. Although it may seem a little outlandish or over religious to look to God, but now since there are over forty thousand deaths worldwide and climbing, we as a people have nothing to lose by turning to God. If we, as a people, would turn to God, we would not have to worry about this invisible enemy, because God has ALWAYS been the

INVISIBLE GOD. In the Good Book, John 1:18 (KJV) says, "No man hath seen God at any time; the only begotten Son, which is in the bosom of the Father, he hath declared him." Again, God is invisible, and an invisible GOD can certainly handle an invisible enemy (COVID 19).

What are you suggesting is the cure for this Coronavirus? Please allow me to explain this to you. In the Word of God, every time God's people committed the sin of taking other things of this world and making them Gods, God became angry and sent a plague. These sicknesses and diseases in Moses' time were called plagues, but now they are called viruses.

You see, the Children of Israel, who like us, were also called God's bride.....were in bondage......in slavery, and they cried out through prayer to God. He heard them and after approximately 346 years, God sent a savior to deliver them from slavery. His name was Moses. God spoke to Moses and told him to go tell Pharaoh to let his people go, so

7.

they could journey out into the wilderness to worship Him. God hardened the heart of the Pharaoh and he refused to do it. So God sent several plagues (viruses in unusual destructive forms) on the Egyptians; He sent frogs, lice, swarms of flies; he killed the cattle, the horses, the asses, the camels, the oxen and the sheep; He put boils on the Egyptians and the beast; he sent pestilence, hail stones with fire mingled among it, that killed man and beast throughout the land of Egypt; He sent locust to eat up everything that was left from the hail stones......getting man's attention, but Pharaoh's heart was still hardened. After this, God sent darkness over all the land of Egypt where they could not even see one another, then God sent a death angel throughout Egypt that killed the firstborn of every Egyptian family, including the firstborn of the maidservants and the firstborn of every animal in Egypt.

When Moses knew what God was going to do with the death angel, he told the Isrealites to take a lamb and kill it; and put the blood on the two side post and the upper door post of every Israelian home, because the Lord would pass over their homes. The Lord did pass through the land of Egypt with the death angel, but whenever He would see the blood of the lamb, He would passover the houses of the Israelites. To this day, that is referred to as the Passover...referring to the day the Lord passed over the houses of the Isrealites because He saw the blood. There were screams that night everywhere in the Egyptian homes as they discovered their firstborn was dead.

After that devastating night for the Egyptians, the Pharaoh released the children of Israel to go out into the wilderness to serve the Lord. Before they left, God softened the hearts of the Egyptians and they allowed the Israelites to borrow the gold and silver from the Egyptians. The Egyptians were the wealthiest people in the land, so the Israelites left out of Egypt extremely rich.

However, when the Pharaoh realized that he had allowed all of his help to leave Egypt, the Paraoh and his army took out after the Israelites. They pursued them to the Red Sea and trapped them. The Red Sea was before the Israelians, the mountains were on their left and right, and Pharaoh and his army were in hot pursuit behind them. What could they do now??? God spoke to Moses and told him to stretch out his rod toward the Red Sea. When he obeyed God, the Red Sea opened up and made a path for the Children of Israel to pass through it. Quite naturally, the bottom of the Red Sea was muddy, so God sent an East wind that blew all night long to dry the bottom of the Red Sea and that allowed the Children of Israel to walk across on dry land. Pharaoh and his army tried to follow the Children of Israel through the Red Sea, but God told Moses to stretch out his rod again, and when he stretched it out again, the Red Sea closed, and that is why you hear people saying, "Pharaoh and his army got drowned in the Red Sea one day." They were all killed that day; but the children of Israel were delivered that day. However, when they finally got out in the wilderness to worship their God, they did like Americans, THEY QUICKLY FORGOT THE LORD!!!

The Lord told Moses to come up on Mount Sinai because He wanted to talk to him. It was there that God wrote the ten commandments on some stones with His finger. However, while God was visiting with Moses, these stiff-necked and stubborn people went to Aaron and told him that they didn't know when this fellow (Moses) was coming back, and they asked him to make them Gods that shall go before them. Aaron told them to bring the gold that they had borrowed from the Egyptians to him. The women as well as the men brought their gold earrings to Aaron. This day and time that we live in is not the first time that men have worn earrings. Then Aaron threw the earrings into the fire, and he melted it down and fashioned it with a graving tool until it it was like a golden calf. Aaron also made an altar so that they could make sacrifices on it. Then the Children of Israel committed a great sin. They started bowing down to this golden calf and worshiping it.

That is when God and even Moses could not take it any longer. God and Moses became extremely angry. Moses picked up the ten commandments that God had written with His own finger and threw them down the mountain breaking them. After that, I believe that God planned to kill all of the Israelites, but before He could do it, Moses convinced God not to, because His enemies would say that He could not deliver His people. So God repented. What does that mean. It means that God changed His mind. God told the Levites to take their swords and go among the people and slay those who had worshiped the idol god, and that day they killed with the sword around 3,000 people....a small pandemic.

And God said unto them, in Exodus 34:12-15 (KJV) "Take heed to thyself, lest thou make a covenant with the inhabitants of the land whither thou goest, lest it be for a snare in the midst of thee: but ye shall destroy their altars, break their images, and cut down their groves: for thou shalt worship no other god: for the LORD, whose name is Jealous, for he is a jealous God: Exodus 34:15 (KJV) Lest thou make a covenant with the inhabitants of the land, and they go a whoring after their gods, and do sacrifice unto their gods, and one call thee, and thou eat of his sacrifice;

You see, God hates it when His creation serves other gods. But God is so compassionate. If His people will repent, God will give them another chance. Exodus 15:26 (KJV) tells us that

9.

God said, "If thou wilt diligently hearken to the voice of the LORD thy God, and wilt do that which is right in his sight, and wilt give ear to his commandments, and keep all his statutes, I will put none of these diseases upon thee....none of these plagues, which I have brought upon the Egyptians: for I am the LORD that healeth thee. Our sin is that we as a nation have

become so arrogant as a people, we have forgotten our creator and we have gone after other Gods. As we study history in the Bible, every nation that forgot God and made other Gods, God sought to destroy it by sending plagues. Again, in the past they were called plagues, but in this day and time they are called viruses. Exodus 32:35 (KJV) says, "And the LORD plagued the people, because they made the calf, which Aaron made."

Deuteronomy 28:1-14 proclaims, " And it shall come to pass, if thou shalt hearken diligently unto the voice of the LORD thy God, to observe and to do all his commandments which I command thee this day, that the LORD thy God will set thee on high above all nations of the earth:

(Deu 28:2 KJV) And all these blessings shall come on thee, and overtake thee, if thou shalt hearken unto the voice of the LORD thy God.

(Deu 28:3 KJV) Blessed shalt thou be in the city, and blessed shalt thou be in the field.

(Deu 28:4 KJV) Blessed shall be the fruit of thy body, and the fruit of thy ground, and the fruit of thy cattle, the increase of thy kind, and the flocks of thy sheep.
(Deu 28:5 KJV) Blessed shall be thy basket and thy store.
(Deu 28:6 KJV) Blessed shalt thou be when thou comest in, and blessed shalt thou be when thou goest out.

(Deu 28:7 KJV) The LORD shall cause thine enemies that rise up against thee to be smitten before thy face: they shall come out against thee one way, and flee before thee seven ways.

(Deu 28:8 KJV) The LORD shall command the blessing upon thee in thy storehouses, and in all that thou settest thine hand unto; and he shall bless thee in the land which the LORD thy God giveth thee.

(Deu 28:9 KJV) The LORD shall establish thee an holy people unto himself, as he hath sworn unto thee, if thou shalt keep the commandments of the LORD thy God, and walk in his ways.

(Deu 28:10 KJV) And all people of the earth shall see that thou art called by the name of the

10.

LORD; and they shall be afraid of thee.
(Deu 28:11 KJV) And the LORD shall make thee plenteous in goods, in the fruit of thy body, and in the fruit of thy cattle, and in the fruit of thy ground, in the land which the LORD sware unto thy fathers to give thee.

(Deu 28:12 KJV) The LORD shall open unto thee his good treasure, the heaven to give the rain unto thy land in his season, and to bless all the work of thine hand: and thou shalt lend unto many nations, and thou shalt not borrow.

(Deu 28:13 KJV) And the LORD shall make thee the head, and not the tail; and thou shalt be above only, and thou shalt not be beneath; if that thou hearken unto the commandments of the LORD thy God, which I command thee this day, to observe and to do them:

(Deu 28:14 KJV) And thou shalt not go aside from any of the words which I command thee this day, to the right hand, or to the left, to go after other gods to serve them.

However, look at Deuteronomy 28:15-68 (KJV). It proclaims, ". . . If thou wilt NOT hearken unto the voice of the LORD thy God, to observe to do all his commandments and his statutes which I command thee this day; that all these curses shall come upon thee, and overtake thee:

(Deu 28:16 KJV) Cursed shalt thou be in the city, and cursed shalt thou be in the field.
(Deu 28:17 KJV) Cursed shall be thy basket and thy store.

(Deu 28:18 KJV) Cursed shall be the fruit of thy body, and the fruit of thy land, the increase of thy kind, and the flocks of thy sheep.

(Deu 28:19 KJV) Cursed shalt thou be when thou comest in, and cursed shalt thou be when thou goest out.

(Deu 28:20 KJV) The LORD shall send upon thee cursing, vexation, and rebuke, in all that thou settest thine hand unto for to do, until thou be destroyed, and until thou perish quickly; because of the wickedness of thy doings, whereby thou hast forsaken me.

(Deu 28:21 KJV) The LORD shall make the pestilence cleave unto thee, until he have consumed thee from off the land, whither thou goest to possess it.

(Deu 28:22 KJV) The LORD shall smite thee with a consumption, and with a fever, and with an inflammation, and with an extreme burning, and with the sword, and with blasting, and with mildew; and they shall pursue thee until thou perish.

11.

(Deu 28:23 KJV) And thy heaven that is over thy head shall be brass, and the earth that is under thee shall be iron.

Deu 28:24 (KJV) The LORD shall make the rain of thy land powder and dust: from heaven shall it come down upon thee, until thou be destroyed.

(Deu 28:25 KJV) The LORD shall cause thee to be smitten before thine enemies: thou shalt go out one way against them, and flee seven ways before them: and shalt be removed into all the kingdoms of the earth.

(Deu 28:26 KJV) And thy carcase shall be meat unto all fowls of the air, and unto the beasts of the earth, and no man shall fray them away.

(Deu 28:27 KJV) The LORD will smite thee with the botch of Egypt, and with the emerods, and with the scab, and with the itch, whereof thou canst not be healed.

(Deu 28:28 KJV) The LORD shall smite thee with madness, and blindness, and astonishment of heart:

(Deu 28:29 KJV) And thou shalt grope at noonday, as the blind gropeth in darkness, and thou shalt not prosper in thy ways: and thou shalt be only oppressed and spoiled evermore, and no man shall save thee.

(Deu 28:30 KJV) Thou shalt betroth a wife, and another man shall lie with her: thou shalt build an house, and thou shalt not dwell therein: thou shalt plant a vineyard, and shalt not gather the grapes thereof.

(Deu 28:31 KJV) Thine ox shall be slain before thine eyes, and thou shalt not eat thereof: thine ass shall be violently taken away from before thy face, and shall not be restored to thee: thy sheep shall be given unto thine enemies, and thou shalt have none to rescue them.

(Deu 28:32 KJV) Thy sons and thy daughters shall be given unto another people, and thine eyes shall look, and fail with longing for them all the day long: and there shall be no might in thine hand.

(Deu 28:33 KJV) The fruit of thy land, and all thy labours, shall a nation which thou knowest not eat up; and thou shalt be only oppressed and crushed alway:

(Deu 28:34 KJV) So that thou shalt be mad for the sight of thine eyes which thou shalt see.

12.

(Deu 28:35 KJV) The LORD shall smite thee in the knees, and in the legs, with a sore botch that cannot be healed, from the sole of thy foot unto the top of thy head.

(Deu 28:36 KJV) The LORD shall bring thee, and thy king which thou shalt set over thee, unto a nation which neither thou nor thy fathers have known; and there shalt thou serve other gods, wood and stone.

(Deu 28:37 KJV) And thou shalt become an astonishment, a proverb, and a byword, among all nations whither the LORD shall lead thee.

(Deu 28:38 KJV) Thou shalt carry much seed out into the field, and shalt gather but little in; for the locust shall consume it.

(Deu 28:39 KJV) Thou shalt plant vineyards, and dress them, but shalt neither drink of the wine, nor gather the grapes; for the worms shall eat them.

(Deu 28:40 KJV) Thou shalt have olive trees throughout all thy coasts, but thou shalt not anoint thyself with the oil; for thine olive shall cast his fruit.

(Deu 28:41 KJV) Thou shalt beget sons and daughters, but thou shalt not enjoy them; for they shall go into captivity.

(Deu 28:42 KJV) All thy trees and fruit of thy land shall the locust consume.

(Deu 28:43 KJV) The stranger that is within thee shall get up above thee very high; and thou shalt come down very low.

(Deu 28:44 KJV) He shall lend to thee, and thou shalt not lend to him: he shall be the head, and thou shalt be the tail.

(Deu 28:45 KJV) Moreover all these curses shall come upon thee, and shall pursue thee, and overtake thee, till thou be destroyed; because thou hearkenedst not unto the voice of the LORD thy God, to keep his commandments and his statutes which he commanded thee:

(Deu 28:46 KJV) And they shall be upon thee for a sign and for a wonder, and upon thy seed for ever.

(Deu 28:47 KJV) Because thou servedst not the LORD thy God with joyfulness, and with gladness of heart, for the abundance of all things;

13.

(Deu 28:48 KJV) Therefore shalt thou serve thine enemies which the LORD shall send against thee, in hunger, and in thirst, and in nakedness, and in want of all things: and he shall put a yoke of iron upon thy neck, until he have destroyed thee.

(Deu 28:49 KJV) The LORD shall bring a nation against thee from far, from the end of the earth, as swift as the eagle flieth; a nation whose tongue thou shalt not understand;

(Deu 28:50 KJV) A nation of fierce countenance, which shall not regard the person of the old, nor show favour to the young:

(Deu 28:51 KJV) And he shall eat the fruit of thy cattle, and the fruit of thy land, until thou be destroyed: which also shall not leave thee either corn, wine, or oil, or the increase of thy kine, or flocks of thy sheep, until he have destroyed thee.

(Deu 28:52 KJV) And he shall besiege thee in all thy gates, until thy high and fenced walls come down, wherein thou trustedst, throughout all thy land: and he shall besiege thee in all thy gates throughout all thy land, which the LORD thy God hath given thee.

(Deu 28:53 KJV) And thou shalt eat the fruit of thine own body, the flesh of thy sons and of thy daughters, which the LORD thy God hath given thee, in the siege, and in the straitness, wherewith thine enemies shall distress thee:

(Deu 28:54 KJV) So that the man that is tender among you, and very delicate, his eye shall be evil toward his brother, and toward the wife of his bosom, and toward the remnant of his children which he shall leave:

(Deu 28:55 KJV) So that he will not give to any of them of the flesh of his children whom he shall eat: because he hath nothing left him in the siege, and in the straitness, wherewith thine enemies shall distress thee in all thy gates.

(Deu 28:56 KJV) The tender and delicate woman among you, which would not adventure to set the sole of her foot upon the ground for delicateness and tenderness, her eye shall be evil toward the husband of her bosom, and toward her son, and toward her daughter,

(Deu 28:57 KJV) And toward her young one that cometh out from between her feet, and toward her children which she shall bear: for she shall eat them for want of all things secretly in the siege and straitness, wherewith thine enemy shall distress thee in thy gates.

14.

(Deu 28:58-59 KJV) If thou wilt not observe to do all the words of this law that are written in this book, that thou mayest fear this glorious and fearful name, THE LORD THY GOD; Then the LORD will make thy plagues wonderful, and the plagues of thy seed, even great plagues, and of long continuance, and sore sicknesses, and of long continuance.

(Deu 28:60 KJV) Moreover he will bring upon thee all the diseases of Egypt, which thou wast afraid of; and they shall cleave unto thee.

(Deu 28:61 KJV) Also every sickness, and every plague, which is not written in the book of this law, them will the LORD bring upon thee, until thou be destroyed.

(Deu 28:62 KJV) And ye shall be left few in number, whereas ye were as the stars of heaven for multitude; because thou wouldest not obey the voice of the LORD thy God.

(Deu 28:63 KJV) And it shall come to pass, that as the LORD rejoiced over you to do you good, and to multiply you; so the LORD will rejoice over you to destroy you, and to bring you to nought; and ye shall be plucked from off the land whither thou goest to possess it.

(Deu 28:64 KJV) And the LORD shall scatter thee among all people, from the one end of the earth even unto the other; and there thou shalt serve other gods, which neither thou nor thy fathers have known, even wood and stone.

(Deu 28:65 KJV) And among these nations shalt thou find no ease, neither shall the sole of thy foot have rest: but the LORD shall give thee there a trembling heart, and failing of eyes, and sorrow of mind:

(Deu 28:66 KJV) And thy life shall hang in doubt before thee; and thou shalt fear day and night, and shalt have none assurance of thy life:

(Deu 28:67-68 KJV) In the morning thou shalt say, Would God it were even! and at even thou shalt say, Would God it were morning! for the fear of thine heart wherewith thou shalt fear, and for the sight of thine eyes which thou shalt see. (Deu 28:68 KJV) And the LORD shall bring thee into Egypt again with ships, by the way whereof I spake unto thee, Thou shalt see it no more again: and there ye shall be sold unto your enemies for bondmen and bondwomen, and no man shall buy you."

God is very specific concerning His blessings and curses. This especially holds true when His people forget Him and make other gods.

CHAPTER II
MR. PRESIDENT
GOD IS WAITING ON YOU

Mr. President, I am praying that Instead of trying to invent the wheel and saying that this has never happened before, why can't you as our national leader try something that already works....we have tried everything else. Many Americans have tried prayer and they know that prayer works.

Mr. President, GOD is waiting on 'you'. 'You' have the ear of the world. We know that you are the leader of America, but some call you the leader of the world, because America is the most powerful nation in the world.

The ball is in your court, Mr. President. Suppose our President, President Trump, instead of having an update briefing in front of the world wide news cameras giving the American people news of how quickly this Coronavirus is spreading, suppose President Trump would ask all Americans and every leader of other countries in the world to join him in a word of prayer for the world; and he would kneel down and pray a prayer something like this:

"Heavenly Father, we humble ourselves before you, as leaders and people of every kindred and nation, Father we admit that we need 'YOUR' help. Please hear us as we turn our faces to you. We confess that we have sinned for we have allowed other people and things in our world to become gods. Please forgive us. We acknowledge that you alone are God and that you have all power over everything. Thank you for using the Coronavirus to get our attention all over the world. O God, again please forgive us of all our sins. We turn our faces to you oh God, and we ask you to take this Coronavirus out of the world....and when you do, we will never ever again forget that you alone are God, and we will not be ashamed to worship and honor you, or afraid to call your glorious and precious name.

Thank you God for hearing our prayers, and thank you again for forgiving our sins. We pray in the name of your darling son, Jesus. Amen."

Again, 2 Chronicles 7:14 says, "(2 Chr 7:14 KJV) If my people, which are called by my name, shall humble themselves, and pray, and seek my face, and turn from their wicked ways; then will I hear from heaven, and will forgive

16.

their sin, and will heal their land."

If our President would lead us all over the world in a prayer like that, something would happen! God would forgive our sins and I believe we would see a change all over the WORLD!!!

CHAPTER III
HISTORY GIVES US EXAMPLES

I repeat, this is not the first time we on this earth have faced a pandemic. A pandemic is judgment or a disease prevalent over a whole country or on the known world. History records that this has happened at least several times....and it happened all because man forgot GOD and because of man's sins. Some entire cities and even nations have been destroyed; and each time these counties recovered, it was because they repented:

1. Gen. 19 In Sodom and Gamorah there was a pandemic and the entire world was wiped out. God looked down on Sodom and Gomorah and sin was running rampant upon the earth, and God sent two angels to tell Lott to take his wife and family and leave the city because he was going to destroy it because of their sin. God rained down fire and brimstone upon Sodom and Gomorrah and destroyed both cities entirely because of their sins. Hundreds of thousands died. Only Lott and his family escaped. In the Word of God, many times when God was trying to get the attention of people, He sent a plague. Please allow me to give you a few other examples:
2. When the Pharaoh in Egypt would not let God's people go into the wilderness to worship God, He sent many plagues on the Pharaoh and the people of Egypt. It was the only known area of the earth then, and there was a pandemic everywhere.
3. Noah, preached to the known world, "It's going to rain".........a pandemic is coming," but they laughed at him. Finally God allowd it to rain and it destroyed the entire world. When the Children of Israel complained about not having any meat to eat, after all God had done to free them from slavery, Numbers 10:33 says, "And while the flesh was yet between their teeth, ere it was chewed, the wrath of the LORD was kindled against the people, and the LORD smote the people with a very great plague."
4. In 1 Samuel 4-6, God sent emerods on the people and destroyed many of them because of their sin. They set the Ark of the Covenant which represented our God, beside their so called god, 'Dagon', and the next morning he was found face down with his head and hands cut off. God's sent a pandemic against those people so they were destroyed.

5. In Numbers 16:41 (KJV), when all the congregation of the children of Israel murmured against his servant Moses and against Aaron , saying, "Ye have killed the people of the LORD," God became angry and started a plague among them; and before Moses and Aaron could offer an atonement for their sins, God had allowed over 14,700 of them to be killed from the plague. Needless to say, this cause a pandemic all over the land. When Aaron returned unto Moses unto the door of the tabernacle of the congregation, the plague was stayed....God stopped the plague. I believe God is trying to get our attention in this world, and God would stop this Coronavirus if the world would only repent of their sins and about forgetting God and accepting other gods....

We as a people in America have made other gods out of almost everything. It's alright to honor Sports figures, but when we make them gods and start bowing to them, we have gone too far. Sports figures (football players, basketball players, baseball players, hockey players are talented, but I have seen on television people stand up in the stands, raise their hands straight up in the air and bow down before them, after they run a piece of pig skin over a goal line, or dunk a basketball into a net. They would not even be able to run, had not GOD given them the strength. God gave man the ability to make money at The US Mint in Washington D. C; but instead of giving God the glory, man turned around and made the money a god. God is trying to get man attention. Deuteronomy 5:7 (KJV) declares "Thou shalt have none other gods before me." Jeremiah 25:6 (KJV) says, "And go not after other godsto serve them, and to worship them, and provoke me not to anger with the works of your hands; and I will do you no hurt."

CHAPTER IV
DON'T FAINT!!!

Please say this confession to yourself, or out loud if you would like: "God said that He wishes above all things that I would prosper and be in health, even as my soul prospers. Today, I shall read a Word that will help me prosper. I will not only be a hearer of the Word, but also a doer of the Word; and I shall go up up up up, up up up up!!!! ! In JESUS name I decree and declare this. Amen." Now if you believe that give GOD a real shout!!!! Galations 6:9 (KJV) says, "And let us not be weary in well doing: for in due season we shall
 reap, if we faint not." If we don't faint. That is the stipulation. We must not faint. America

18.

as a country has done a lot of good for it's people and for others around the world. We can see this good come back to us if we don't faint.

It would be so wonderful if all American would become people who encourage each other. Hebrews 10:25 (KJV) declares, "Not forsaking the assembling of ourselves together, as the manner of some is; but exhorting one another: and so much the more, as ye see the day approaching. What day approaching? The day of the Lord approaching. The Lord is on His way back. This may shock you, but I believe that the Lord is going to come back in our lifetime.

I believe that one day, just like the Bible declares it, God will put one foot on the land and one foot in the sea and declare that time will be no more. The trumpet shall sound so loud that everyone on earth will hear it. The incredullities of life shall be no more.

And I want to do this because that is exactly what the enemy is trying to get...all of the saints to do. He wants all of us to faint! Because the enemy knows that in due season we shall reap our blessings......if.........................we faint not. Everyone wants to be blessed, so don't faint. Your blessing is on the way. Hang on in there.....and again, don't faint. Don't give up and don't give in. I believe you are next in line for a blessing. If you believe that, say these words after me in your heart, or out loud:

1. The enemy is trying to make me faint, because he knows that if I don't give up, I will reap my blessings.
2. So I've got to hang on in there.
3. Even if I have hard trials and great tribulations,
4. Whatever I do, I cannot faint; because my due season is coming, and the blessing is on the way. Now, if you believe that, don't wait til the battle is over. If you are not ashamed, give GOD a great shout now!!!!!

If there has ever been a time when God's people need to be encouraged....I believe the time is now! This is NOT the time to give up, and this is NOT the time to throw in the towel. Our due season is almost here. How do you know that! Because things are getting frantic......so frantic that people don't know what to do....and when you don't know what to do, just hold on! Be strong! It's going to be alright. We are coming out of this stressful time with our hands up, if we don't faint.

In 2Kings, the 5th chapter, the odds were stacked against Naaman. He was the captain of the

19.

host for the King of Syria. It was known that He was a great man with his master, and honorable, because through him, the LORD had defeated Syria: he was also a mighty man in valor; but he had a problem....he had leprosy. There were forces all in his mind trying to get Naaman to faint. For leprosy was a vicious and vile disease. It could get so bad it might rot your hand or foot off, and there was no known cure for it just like the Coronavirus.

But Naaman heard through a little maid from the land of Israel that waited on Naaman's wife, that there was a prophet down in Samaria who could cure him of leprosy. She said unto her mistress, " Would God my lord were with the prophet that is in Samaria! for he would recover him of his leprosy."

When Elisha the prophet heard about Naaman, after some procedures of protocol, he allowed Naaman to come that he should know that there is a prophet in Israel. Naaman departed, and took with him ten talents of silver, and six thousand pieces of gold, and ten changes of raiment. He finally made it to the prophets door, and stood with his horses and with his chariot; but instead of Elisha the prophet being cordial and coming out to him, he simply sent a messenger unto him, saying, Go and wash in Jordan seven times, and thy flesh shall come again to thee, and thou shalt be clean.

Naaman was furious, and went away, and said, "Behold, I thought, He would surely come out to me, and stand, and call on the name of the LORD his God, and strike his hand over the place, and recover the leper.......Are not Abana and Pharpar, rivers of Damascus, better than all the waters of Israel? may I not wash in them, and be clean? So he turned and went away in a rage."

However, 2 Kings 5:13 says, "...And his servants came near, and spake unto him, and said, My father, if the prophet had bid thee do some great thing, wouldest thou not have done it? how much rather then, when he saith to thee, Wash, and be clean?" Naaman followed the advise of his servant and went down, and dipped himself seven times in the Jordan River, according to the saying of the man of God: and his flesh came back again just like the flesh of a little child, and he was clean of that leprosy.

Naaman was almost about to faint, but when he heard about Elisha the prophet, he got his faith back. It's not a good thing to start fainting. When one starts fainting, at least 3 things will start happening to them:

1. Good ground will be lost. When you are making good ground like America was making, evil forces seem to get jealous and start working against you. (John 10:10 KJV) The thief cometh not, but for to steal, and to kill, and to destroy: I am come that

20.

   they might have life, and that they might have it more abundantly. Evil forces want people to faint so he can steal, kill and destroy them.
   2. It sets one up for future defeats......fainting is a spirit and it will try to get in your demeanor......when evil forces gets you once, they will try to get you twice. It's like if evil forces can get you over here, they feel lie they can get you over there. If you start fainting, next time it will be easier for evil forces to turn you around.

   It is better to believe like the Children of Israel in (2 Chronicles 20:15b KJV) "Be not afraid nor dismayed by reason of this great multitude (the things that you are facing); for the battle is not yours, but God's. None of the battles you are facing are yours anyway. Turn all of them over to the one above. If you don't turn them over to Him, evil forces will set you up for future defeats.
   3. If you faint, the enemy will try to snatch away the blessings that you have worked so hard for: so don't faint!!! America and our Leader has worked so hard to make our country greater, but evil forces desire to snatch them away. Galatians 6:9 (KJV) tells us, "And let us not be weary in well doing: for in due season we shall reap, if we faint not." Let us not faint!!!"

Genesis 1:26 (KJV) says, "And God said, Let us make man in our image, after our likeness: and let them have dominion over the fish of the sea, and over the foul of the air, and over the cattle, and over all the earth, "and over every creeping thing that creepeth upon the earth." Listen, the Coronavirus is a creeping thing upon this earth, and according to Genesis 1:26, God ordered that we (the creation of God) would have dominion (authority) on this planet earth.....not evil forces....WE have it.....!!!!!!!!!!!!......men and women who love GOD.

But listen, evil forces are trying to use everything they can to make us think that 'they' have dominion over 'us' and over this earth. But the Word that has been tested and proven says that GOD gave the dominion to US. Now who's report will you believe...............Whatever your problem is......it does not have dominion over 'you'. 'You' have dominion over it, no matter what the problem is, GOD gave 'you' dominion over it. I want to name at least 60 things that the enemy uses to make us think that 'he' has dominion over us, instead of us having dominion over the evil forces of this world.

   1. Cancer.........cancer is the most arrogant disease I know of. It will try to make people believe that once you get it, there is no hope or cure for you........but there are cases after cases that prove that we have dominion over cancer....they had cancer but now they are cancer free.....we have dominion over cancer!!!! We have dominion over:
   2. Prostrate cancer

21.
3. Cervical cancer
4. Stomach cancer
5. Throat cancer
6. Brain cancer
7. Brest cancer
8. Pancreatic cancer
9. Liver cancer
10. Bone cancer, and any kind of cancer
11. Diabetes...it has been proven that we have dominion over it.
12. High blood...it has been proven that we have dominion over it.
13. Low blood...it has been proven that we have dominion over it.
14. Carpal Tunnel Syndrome...it has been proven....
15. Strokes...it has been proven....
16. Heart problems......heart attacks...it has been proven....
17. Asthma...it has been proven....
18. Gout......it has been proven that we have dominion over it..
19. Kidney problems...it has been proven....
20. Cataracks...it has been proven....
21. COPD (Chronic Obstruction Pulmonary Disease)....people needing oxygen...it has been proven....
22. Money...it has been proven....
23. Gum Abscesses...it has been proven....
24. Inner Ear Infection (& aches)...it has been proven....
25. Dizziness...it has been proven....
26. Sinus infections......it has been proven....
27. Sinus drips...it has been proven....
28. Coughing...it has been proven....
29. Sore Throat...it has been proven....
30. Ulcers...it has been proven....
31. Brain Tumor...it has been proven....
32. He-cups...it has been proven....
33. Panic Attacks ...it has been proven....
34. Fear...it has been proven....
35. Impatient feelings...it has been proven....
36. Chronic Pain Attacks...it has been proven....
37. Chronic Back Pains...it has been proven....
38. Chronic Arthritis Pains...it has been proven....
39. Chronic Headaches...it has been proven....
40. Chronic Feet Pain...it has been proven....
41. Chronic Leg Pain...it has been proven....

42. Chronic Neck Pain...it has been proven....
43. Chronic Arm Pain...it has been proven....
44. Hip Pain (Hip slipping out of the socket)...it has been proven....
45. Chronic Side Pain...it has been proven....
46. Chronic Stomach Pain...it has been proven....
47. Chronic Knee Pain & any kind of chronic pa...it has been proven....
48. Chronic tiredness...it has been proven....
49. Joint Paint (shoulders & hips)...it has been proven....
50. Depression......it has been proven that we have dominion over it. Side Affects From Prescription Drugs & Medicines.......it has been proven....
51. Lupus...it has been proven....
52. Cycle Cell Anemia...it has been proven....
53. Occurring Boils on your body...it has been proven....
54. Amputations...it has been proven....
55. Flu...........it has been proven that we have dominion over it.
56. Pneumonia......it has been proven that we have dominion over it.
57. Kidney Problems...it has been proven....
58. Anxiety Attacks, ...it has been proven....
59. Crones Disease...it has been proven....
60. D'Andre Syndrome...it has been proven....
61. Blood Clots......it has been proven that we have dominion over it.
62. Mussel Spasms...it has been proven that we have dominion over it.
63. THE Coronavirus.....IT'S A CREEPING THING AND WE HAVE DOMINION OVER EVERY CREEPING THING.

No matter what our problem may be, let us close our eyes and in the Spirit realm, see ourselves over-comers above all these problems including this Carona Virus. Let us us open your mouth and speak it out loud by faith, "Our nation is healed".... Then those who have it or
have friends that have it, say, "I am healed, and say "My love ones are healed!!!" By faith, keep saying it every day, and then give the anointing time to work......I don't care how you feel...you are not healed by your feelings. You are healed by your faith! Say it by faith every day, "I'm healed."........and if you will keep loosing that on earth and give the anointing time to work, in due seadon, you will see a great change....it will materialize in the natural! You have dominion over that thing.......it's on the earth isn't it. GOD, GOD who created that thing for His glory, gave YOU dominion over that thing.

Many times evil forces tries to use negative things to make us think that 'he' has dominion over us, rather than 'you' having dominion over that thing.......but the enemy IS a liar. 'You', you, you, you, 'YOU', have dominion over that thing and the evil forces too, because that

23,

dominion was given to you by GOD Himself. The evil forces are just trying to use these things to steal your dominion. The evil forces in this world want your dominion.

They are trying to do the same thing he tried to do up in heaven. According to history of evil forces, in Rev. 12:9, evil forces got kicked out of heaven because they were trying to get dominion in heaven: but they failed and got kicked out of heaven by God's angels; but those evil forces landed down here on earth where we are. The enemy is a thief!!!! Now he's trying to deceive 'us here on earth' and trick us into giving up our dominion down here on earth.....because 'the enemy' wants it. According to Revelations 12:4, He deceived 1/3 of the heavenly host up in heaven. That's 33 1/3 million angels according to Revelations 5:11. The enemy and his angels lost the battle up in heaven. He and his angels were kicked out of heaven and they fell down here to earth. Revelations 12:12 says, "Woe to the inhabitants of the earth." Now the enemy is trying to deceive 'you' here on earth' and steal your dominion; but don't let him do it!

GOD said it's your dominion, not evil forces!!!! The enemy comes to steal, but don't let him steal your dominion from 'you'!

CHAPTER V

WORSHIP POSITIONS

While we are going through this pandemic, we need to pray; and when we pray, I think we need to know that there are certain worship positions that have a specific meaning to God:

1. **Standing**...a Position of honoring the Lord and His Word by standing. (Psa 134:1 KJV) ".......Behold, bless ye the LORD, all ye servants of the LORD, <u>which by night stand in the house of the LORD</u>. When you stand, you honor His Word, and God's Word is God. (Psalms 135:1 (KJV) Praise ye the LORD. Praise ye the name of the LORD; praise him, O ye servants of the LORD.
2. **Kneeling**...a position of humbleness...it means that you humble yourself before God.
3. **Hands lifted up**...a position of surrendering all.
4. **Head bowed**...a position of giving reverence and respect
5. **Hands folded**...a worshipful position

6. **Stubbornness....** a position of stubbornness or being rebellious..... your worship position can reveal this. People go to the dentist and when the dentist says, "Open your mouth", you open it. People go to the doctor, and when the doctor ask the person to take off all their clothes and get upon the table they do it. But when people come to church and the man of God ask them to stand, some people won't stand, and they won't lift their hands....they won't bow before God, but they are willing to bow before some Olympic heroes or some sports figures....some football, basketball or baseball players. This is rebellion toward God.. You are willing to idolize someone talented as an American idol, but they are stubborn to honor GOD!

Psalms 5:5 KJV) says, "The foolish shall not stand in thy sight: thou hatest all workers of iniquity." People are willing to do whatever stars tell them to do, but When the Lord tells them to do something, they won't do it. This symbolizes rebellion and stubbornness.........(1 Samuel 15:23 KJV) tells us, "For rebellion is as the sin of witchcraft, and stubbornness is as iniquity and idolatry. Because thou hast rejected the word of the LORD, he hath also rejected thee."

7. **Facial expression..your heart...and voice**.........The expression on your face.....the sentiments of your heart, and voice. These positions many times can reveal that you are <u>desperate</u> for the move of God..... Listen, your face and your heart may show the real desires of your heart.... in worship, your facial expressions and many times the sound of your voice can reveal it.....when you say "I love you Lord", people can look at you and see whether or not you mean it.....they can see it on your face and feel it from your heart and even hear it in your voice that you truly love the Lord, and that you are desperate for God to move. David said in Psalms 84:2 (KJV) "My soul longeth, yea, even fainteth for the courts of the LORD: my heart and my flesh crieth out for the living God." When you get desperate for GOD, many times, tears stream down your face. You cry out before Him. Psalms 42:1 (KJV) David proclaims, "...As the hart panteth after the water brooks, so panteth my soul after thee, O God.

Psalms 42:2 KJV) "My soul thirsteth for God, for the living God." The Apostle Paul said in (Phil 3:10 KJV) "That I may know him, and the power of his resurrection, and . the fellowship of his sufferings, being made conformable unto his death." This is when you are desperate for God and want to know Him.

25.

PLAGUES:

In the Word of God, many times when God was trying to get the attention of people, He sent a plague. Please allow me to give you a few examples:

1. When the Pharaoh in Egypt would not let God's people go into the wilderness to worship God, He sent many plagues on the Pharaoh and the people of Egypt.
2. Whenever the people of God worshiped other Gods, God became angry and sent plagues among them:
3. When the Children of Israel complained about not having any meat to eat, after all God had done to free them from slavery, Numbers 10:33 says, "And while the flesh was yet between their teeth, ere it was chewed, the wrath of the LORD was kindled against the people, and the LORD smote the people with a very great plague."
4. Numbers 14:36 (KJV) tells us that when Moses sent men out to search the land that God promised to the Children of Israel, after they returned and made all the congregation to murmur against him, by bringing up a slander upon the land, the Word tells us that they died by the plague before the LORD.
5. In Numbers 16:41 (KJV), when all the congregation of the children of Israel murmured against his servant Moses and against Aaron , saying, "Ye have killed the people of the LORD," God became angry and started a plague among them; and before Moses and Aaron could offer an atonement for their sins, God had allowed over 14,700 of them to be killed from the plague. When Aaron returned unto Moses unto the door of the tabernacle of the congregation, the plague was stayed....God stopped the plague. I believe God is trying to get our attention in this world, and God would stop this Coronavirus if the world would only repent about forgetting God and accepting other gods....

We as a people have made other gods out of almost everything. Sports figures (football players, basketball players, baseball players, hockey players are talented, but I have seen on television people stand up in the stands, raise their hands straight up in the air and bow down before them, after they run a piece of pig skin over a goal line, or dunk a basketball into a net. They

would not even be able to run, had not GOD given them the strength. God gave man the ability to make money at US Mint in Washington D. C; but instead of giving God the glory, man turned around and made the money a god. God is trying to get man attention. Deuteronomy 5:7 (KJV) declares "Thou shalt have none other gods before me." Jeremiah 25:6

(KJV) says, "And go not after other gods to serve them, and to worship them, <u>and provoke me not to anger</u> with the works of your hands; and I will do you no hurt."

CHAPTER VI
THE LIFE IS IN THE BLOOD

Our Lord and savior, Jesus Christ has already shed His blood on Calvary as atonement for all of our sins, but our President may have to call our entire nation to a fast to symbolize to God that we are sorry for our sins. If we would fast, I believe that God would turn this Coronavirus around. Leviticus 17:11 (KJV) tells us "For the life of the flesh is in the blood: and I have given it to you upon the altar to make an atonement for your souls: for it is the blood that maketh an atonement for the soul."

A few months ago, God spoke to my heart and said, "Son, call the sick together on the prayer line, because I'm going to do mass healings on the Prayer Line on Friday morning. I told the people on the Prayer Line, "If you want to be healed, get your mind on Jesus and let your faith go up to a new level."

In this chapter, I want to do a study on blood, and I want to talk to you about "The Life Is In The Blood". There are some things that all of us need to know about blood. This is a rhema word, and some of these things may baffle your mind, so you may want to write some of them down. Our purpose is to help all of you receive healing through the blood of the Lamb. One of the most important facts for all of us to know is that "The life of the flesh is in the blood." Again, the life is in the blood. I want every person to find every scar on your body, both big scars and little scars. Now I want to ask you to think back and remember how you got that scar, how it happened. Now do you remember how that cut, bruise or wound got healed? Did you have to have stitches, did someone put a bandage on it, or did someone put some antiseptic on it, or did that cut just heal by itself. Some of you, if you can remember how you got those scars, you can't remember how or when they went away. All you know is that they have been healed for years.

This revelation that I'm about to reveal was inspired by the Apostle Paul when he wrote in (Phil 3:10 (KJV). "I want to know you Lord, and the power of his resurrection and the

27.

fellowship of your suffering." Isaiah 1:18 says, "Come now, let us reason together." In other words, come now...let us think this thing out together. Listen, I believe that God is the creator of the human body, and He wants me to tell you that when He created the human body, He already put enough healing in the human body to heal any problems that a person might encounter, or might face right now....but you have to learn to activate that healing virtue already in your body through faith in God.

Allow me to try to prove this to you. I can prove this through the Word by asking 1 question. Here is the question, "Who's image where you created in. (Gen 1:26 (KJV) answers that question for us when it says, "And God said, Let us make man in our image, after our likeness:"and since we were created like God, you don't think He put any healing virtue inside us. When Jesus sent His disciples forth, He said in Matthew 10:8 (KJV), "Heal the sick, cleanse the lepers, raise the dead, cast out devils: freely ye have received, freely give."

Then going back to Genesis 1:26, God said, "let them (us) have dominion over the fish of the sea (we have it), and over the foul of the air (we have it), and over the cattle (we have it), and over all the earth (we have it), and over every creeping thing that creepeth upon the earth....and
since that part of the Word is true, why would anyone think that the dominion about creeping things is not true (we have that too).

That is why the Word says, "...whatever you loose on earth shall be loosed in heaven, and whatever you bind on earth, shall be bound in heaven." I have come to tell you that you already have enough healing virtue in your body to heal the problem....just speak the word and have faith in God. In the name of Jesus, "I don't have any diabetes, cycle cell, lupus, cancer, back trouble, knee trouble....I'm not saying that you don't have any pain right now....I'm saying that to activate the healing virtue already inside your body, you have to activate your faith by speaking the words, and by giving the anointing time to work.

In St. John 11:44, I believe that when Jesus spoke to Lazarus (the brother to Mary and Martha) who had died and Jesus went to his grave and said, "...Take ye away the stone; and Martha, the ister of him that was dead, saith unto him, Lord, by this time he stinketh: for he hath been dead four days." When Jesus spoke to him and commanded that he come forth, I believe that Jesus was speaking to his blood, because the life is in the blood. They had not drained all the blood out of his body as they would do in this day and time. So I believe Jesus commanded the blood to live and Lazarus came forth, because the life was in the blood.

When you cut, bruise, or wound yourself, that scar healed because life was in the blood and the enzymes already in your body became consintrated on that wounded area in your body

28.

and cause it to heal. Now it may have been the prayer that caused God to command the enzymes to heal your body, but just look at that wound......it is no longer there. What happened to it? It has been healed. Isaiah 55:3 (KJV) says, "But he was wounded for our transgressions, he was bruised for our iniquities: the chastisement of our peace was upon him; and with his stripes we are healed."

If we look at every person that received their healing through Jesus when He was on this earth. Every one of them had to have faith...faith in who....faith in Jesus; and every one of them who had strong faith in Jesus, were healed. There are 231 scriptures in the Bible on faith? God wants you to be healed God wants you to be healed. Activate your faith in God and let the Lord heal you.

Listen, blood to mankind is extremely important.
    a. We have about 5.6 liters of blood in our body....that's around 6 quarts of blood, and those 6 quarts of blood circulate through our entire body around 3 times every minute. That means In 1 day, the blood travels a total of 12,000 miles—that's four times the distance across the U.S. From coast to coast...New York to LA.
    b. During an average lifetime, the heart pumps about 1 million barrels of blood through the body. That's enough to fill more than 3 supertankers (that's 3 18 Wheelers). When it comes to cells, it's the cells in the body that carry the blood
    c. In an average human body there are between 222 to 242 billion cells produced in our bodies every day.......each of these cells carry blood that sustain life....why? Because, remember the life is in the blood.
    d. And if you think that's amazing.......The brain.....did you know that in our brain <u>alone</u> there are appromately 100 billion neurons (or 'brain cells' in the human brain. To realize how many brain cells that is, if you would count just '1' cell per second, it would take 3,171 years to do that......and just think, all of these 100 billion brain cells need blood that was created by GOD.....and if blood doesn't circulate to these 100 billion brain cells, your brain would not function correctly.....you would not even be able to think...if GOD didn't allow blood to get to your brain cells. It is truly amazing how important the blood in your body truly is.

Listen, out of those 6 quarts of blood in your body....if we lose even 1 quart of your blood, in many cases your doctor might recommend a blood transfusion. Loosing a quart of blood would be like <u>your life slowly slipping away</u>. Why, because life is in the blood. Have you ever noticed, when a person dies, the first thing that the mortician does during the embalming of a human body is remove the blood......and when they remove the blood, all signs of life completely disappear.

29.

I crossed referenced the scripture that tells us, "Life of the flesh is in the blood", and I discovered something so powerful. The Word says in (Gen 1:26 KJV) And God said, Let us make man in our image, after our likeness: and let them have <u>dominion over</u> the fish of the sea, and over the foul of the air, and over the cattle, and over all the earth, and <u>over every creeping thing that creepeth upon the earth</u>.

Here is what I discovered. When forensic scientist or lab techs. examine blood samples under a microscope, they see things that man cannot see with the human eye.....they see things that have life and that creep upon the earth....and guess what some of the things that creep upon the earth are.......they see cancer cells creeping, diabetes cells creeping and even high blood cells creeping upon the earth....low blood cells...lupus....stroke cells....blood diseases, afflictions, sicknesses, flu, Coronavirus....and all things that creep on the earth. What does that mean.....if you believe the Word of God in Gen. 1:26, it means that we have dominion over all these things. The Word says in Gen 1:26 tells us that we have dominion "over every creeping thing that creepeth upon the earth." Dominion means that we reign over it.....we control it.....it must obey us, not, we must obey it......I remind you of Matt. 16:19 & Mat. 18:18 that says, "...whatsoever we bind on earth shall be bound in heaven."

And when I cross referenced the scripture that tells us, "Life of the flesh is in the blood, I discovered something so mighty, so powerful......what happens in the blood....we know that when forinsic scientist examine blood samples under a microscope, they see things that man cannot see.....they see things that have life and that are creeping upon the earth. I want to remind you of something that I shared with you perhaps in another book. The Word says in (Gen 1:26 KJV) And God said, Let us make man in our image, after our likeness: and let them have <u>dominion over</u> the fish of the sea, and over the foul of the air, and over the cattle, and over all the earth, and <u>over every creeping thing that creepeth upon the earth</u>. Some of those creeping things are......cancer is a creeping thing that creepeth upon the earth........when they put other things under the microscope, they see diabetes cells creeping upon the earth......lupus....cycle cell......blood clots.......high blood...low blood.....creeping things that creepeth upon the earth. What does that mean? It means that we....have.....dominion...over all these things....given to us.....by God Himself!!!!!! It means that cancer has no dominion over you....it means that 'you' have dominion over cancer. It means that 'you win!!!!'

Please allow me to say this again, the life is in the blood. That is why I know that when Jesus stepped to the grave-side of Lazarus, He performed and absolute miracle. Lazarus was dead, in the grave and the Bible says that Martha said "Lord, by this time he stinketh, for he has been dead four days." In other words, the blood had already started to dry up. But Jesus stepped to the graveside and called him by name.....and when Jesus called Lazarus by name, I believe that Jesus was speaking to his blood first. Why? Because the life is in the blood.

30.

I believe the first thing in Lazarus' body that was restored, was the blood. Why, because for Lazarus not to have any blood and be alive, would have broken one of 0the laws of creation. So when Jesus called Lazarus he came forth, but it couldn't have been possible for the legs to walk without the flow of blood in his legs. His arms couldn't have moved without blood flowing in his arms, and he certainly couldn't have come forth without blood flowing in his whole body. Why? Again, I tell you "The life is in the blood." If you lose those 6 quarts of blood in your body, you will surely die, because the life is in your blood.

And when we understand how important blood is to man having life....then we can better understand how important the shedding of blood on Calvary was. Without the shedding of blood:

1. We wouldn't have life right now. Jesus shed His blood and gave His life so that we could have eternal life.
2. No wonder Jesus said in (John 6:54 KJV) Whoso eateth my flesh, and drinketh my blood, hath eternal life; and I will raise him up at the last day....because the life is in the blood of Jesus. When you drink the blood of Jesus, it brings life. That's why when you take communion, make sure you drink all of it, because the juice represents the blood of Jesus.....life.
3. Notice that when the centurion pierced Jesus in the side on Calvary, the Bible says in (John 19:34 KJV) But one of the soldiers with a spear pierced his side, and forthwith came there out blood and water. Notice that soon after that Jesus gave up the ghost in this human body. When the soldier pierce Him in the side, out ran blood (or life) and water. But no man took His life....He laid it down.
4. You see, that is why Jesus said unto Thomas when Thomas said, "Lord, we know not whither thou goest; and how can we know the way?" Then in (John 14:6 KJV) Jesus saith unto Thomas, I am the way, the truth, and the life: no man cometh unto the Father, but by me.....meaning what.....meaning that one could only be saved through the blood of Jesus....meaning that Jesus had to shed His blood in order that we might be saved......meaning that no one can get to the Father except through the blood of Jesus. God is holy, and the angels even at the gates of heaven are going to want to know, have you been washed in the blood. You see, you can't get in without being washed in the blood of the lamb.
5. Hebrews 9:22 (KJV) tells us that, "...and without shedding of blood is no remission. No forgiveness of sins....Jesus shed His blood so that we could have eternal life.

As we get ready for prayer and for mass healings, I want you to note something. Whenever any of the diseases try to attack your ody....and...take....people....out....of this world, notice

31.

that the disease always attacks the blood. You see, even diseases know that 'life is in the blood'. The life is in the blood. Again, how does the enemy use so many diseases to try to take people out of this world? He tries to get in the blood system: but in the name of Jesus, we ask the Lord to send healing through the blood of Jesus. "Lord, today, we plead the blood of Jesus against every disease that is attacking the people of God.

In just a moment I am going to pray and I want you who are reading this book to start pleading the blood of Jesus all over the world against this Coronavirus, and I want you to keep pleading the blood of Jesus longer than you have ever done before....don't be ashamed....the devil is going to try to wear you down to get you to stop pleading the blood; but that means that it is affecting him.....and I want you to get every sickness or disease that you, or anybody you know has and plead the resurrection blood of Jesus against it. In Luke the 6th chapter, there was a whole multitude that followed Jesus, and (Luke 6:19 KJV) says, "And the whole multitude sought to touch him: for there went virtue out of him, and healed them all......(Mat 12:15 KJV) says, ".....and great multitudes followed him, and he healed them all;" every kind of sickness and disease and problem was in the multitude, but Jesus healed.....them.......all. That is mass healings. It is scriptural that God can do that.....He's the same yesterday, today and forever more. The Bible says (James 5:14 KJV) "Is any sick among you? let him call for the elders of the church; and let them pray over him, anointing him with oil (if you have some, get your anointed oil and in the name of Jesus, get ready to plead the blood of Jesus.

I challenge every person worldwide. We have tried the doctors and and the scientist, and so far they have failed to stop this pandemic, we have tried the scientist and so far they have failed to stop this virus. My old gray headed mother and grandmother said, "When you have tried everything and everything has failed......try God. Since every thing has failed to stop this Coronavirus, would it be eccentric, bizarre or too religious to try God????

I mentioned to you that in the 12th chapter of Exodus, when God passed through Egypt, the firstborn of every family was killed, including the Pharaoh's family. But the Israelians put the blood of a lamb on their side post and doorpost, and when the death angel saw the blood, he passed over every house in Israel. that had the blood on the doorpost. We need that in America and all over the world too. If you have sinned, you can be forgiven and healed too. (James 5:15 KJV) says, "And the prayer of faith shall save the sick, and the Lord shall raise him up; and if he have committed sins, they shall be forgiven him." Listen, just repent of your sins, and ask God to heal our world and you too.

As I call these sickness and affliction demons out, I want every person reading this book, if you have any blessed oil, in the Spirit realm, I'm going to ask God to let it represent the blood of Jesus; and I want you to place some on every side post and upper doorpost of your house. If you do not have any olive oil, get whatever oil you have no matter what kind it is. I'm asking God to bless it and let every drop have the potency of the Holy Ghost.

Then, as I pray, I want you to help me plead the blood of Jesus against every affliction and disease and ask God for divine healing. If you are in a place where you can do this out loud, I want you to open your mouth and plead the blood of Jesus with great authority!!!! Don't be ashamed. Remember that Matthew 18:18 says, ". . . Whatsoever ye shall bind on earth shall be bound in heaven: and whatsoever ye shall loose on earth shall be loosed in heaven." How do we bind and loose things??? We bind and loose things by speaking things out loud. Our nation and the world is in serious trouble. Please help me plead the blood of JESUS over these afflictions and ask GOD for divine healing for our nation, and the world. I believe that God is going to heal....them all. I'm praying this prayer, "GOD, in your Word you healed everyone in the multitude, and we are asking you, in the name of Jesus, to heal everyone in the multitude on planet earth; and cover them with the blood of Jesus. "Is there anything too hard for God?" Also, please .forgive all of our sins. Let your healing virtue go out, and bring mass healings to us Lord. Father, we plead the blood of Jesus over:

1. Coronavirus...be healed!
2. Diabetes...be healed!
3. Blood clots...be healed!
4. Heart trouble...be healed!
5. Ulcers...be healed!
6. Lung problems....emphacema, asthma, COPD, and all kinds of lung problems....be healed!
7. All kinds of blood problems...be healed!
    a. High Blood...be healed!
    b. Low Blood...be healed!
    c. Blood clots...be healed!
    e. Blood problems—the thinning of the blood...be healed!
    32.

    f. Disease in the blood...be healed!
    g. Transfusion...be healed!
    h. Blood Purification....dialysis...be healed!
    i. The Issue of blood...be healed!
    j. Aides...be healed!
    k. Cancer...be healed!
        1. Prostrate Cancer...be healed!
        2. Cervical Cancer...be healed

33.

    3. Brain Cancer...be healed!
    4. Colon Cancer...be healed!
    5. Bone Cancer...be healed!
    6. Pancreatic Cancer...be healed!
    8. In the small intestines...be healed!
    9. In the large intestines...be healed!
    10. In the large intestines...be healed!
    11. In the large intestines...be healed!
    12. In the large intestines...be healed!
    13. Breast Cancer...be healed!
    14. Throat Cancer...be healed!
    1t. Pancreatic Cancer...be healed!
    16. Brain Cancer...be healed!
    17. Leukemia...be healed!.
    18. Cycle Cell...be healed!
    19. Lupus...be healed!
    20. Leukemia...be healed!

And any other types of cancer that I didn't call out. God gave dominion over 'you'...be healed!

[(and we also take authority over:)]
    a. Gangrene in the foot & leg ...be healed!
    b. Gout in the joints...be healed!
    c. Lipodemia...be healed!
    d. Swollen Gland problems...be healed!
    e. Varicose Veins...be healed!
    f. All blockage in the legs...be healed!
    g. All blood clots forming— Tumors in that chest...be healed!
    h. Tumors in the stomach—you mass in that stomach...be healed!
    i. Tumors in the lower intestines...be healed!
    j. Blood clots in the feet & legs...be healed
    k. Blood clots in the brain...be healed!
    l. Brain disorders...be healed!
       Swelling in the brain...be healed!
       Brain decay ...be healed!
    m. Mass on the brain...be healed!
    n. Strokes...be healed!

Isaiah 53:5 (KJV) says, "But he was wounded for our transgressions, he was bruised for our iniquities: the chastisement of our peace was upon him; and with his stripes we are healed." In the name of Jesus, we bind these things and proclaim that we do not have any of them. Again, the Word says, "Whatever we bind on earth shall be bound in heaven. So please speak this with me? We speak the things that be not as though they were. In the name of JESUS, we speak that we don't have any of these afflictions:

I speak strength in those hands
I speak strength in those legs
I speak strength in those arms!
I speak strength in those shoulders!
I speak strength in those lungs!
I speak strength in that heart!
I speak that blood clots are dissolve!
Feet................be healed!
Lungs..............be healed!
Brain...............be healed!
Mind...............be healed!
Heart...............be healed!
Eyes................be healed!
Ears.................be healed!
Coronavirus....be healed!

I speak strength to that body! I speak that you shall live & not die!

In the name of Jesus and in the Spirit realm, the blood is flowing throughout your body and we are healed by the blood of Jesus. Can anyone reading this book believe this with me....... I plead the blood of Jesus: Be healed!!!!!!!

o. In the colon, around that liver and In the chest
p. Boils and tumors under the arms! Loose!!!! Migraine headaches!
q. Loose!!!!! Be healed!!!!!!!

As I close this chapter, may I ask you a question? "Do you want to live and not die?"

Remember that when Jesus Christ gave His life on Calvary, He shed His blood so that you might have life....for the life of the flesh is in the blood. For he not only died for sins, but through His blood He also died for sicknesses and diseases. His losing His life made it possible for us to have life.....He gave up the life in His body, so that we could have life in our

35.

body on this earth, and also that we might have eternal life.....for the life is in the blood.

I mentioned earlier that there is already healing virtue in your body. Enzymes. You just have to activate them. How? Through faith.....through believing in GOD. Matthew 17:20 tells us, "... for verily I say unto you, If ye have faith as a grain of mustard seed, ye shall say unto this mountain, Remove hence to yonder place; and it shall remove; <u>and nothing shall be impossible unto you</u>. Enzymes are already in your body..... healing is already in your body.....you just have to believe GOD. That activates it.....and causes your body to be in a state of hope, and "we are saved by hope."

One of the purposes of this chapter is to help all of us understand the blood more, in order to better understand the importance of what the shedding of blood on Calvary truly meant and means right now.

In (Exo 19:10 KJV), God said unto Moses, "Go unto the people, and sanctify them to day and to morrow, and let them wash their clothes"......then He said concerning timing in vs 11, "And be ready against the third day: for the third day the LORD will come down upon Mount Sinai in the sight of all the people." "The Lord spoke to my heart and inspired me to believe that He can do mass healings, and it is all due to the shedding of the blood of Jesus.

CHAPTER VII
THANK GOD FOR YOUR SIGNS

Thank God for the signs, because it's the signs that lead to miracles that give us more hope. I'm a little concerned, because I know that even though God is doing some incredible things for 'you', and there are signs all around 'you', some people just can't see them. I believe God wants me to give the people who are going through and who are reading this book this message. The message is this, "Thank God for the signs". God gives us so many signs to show us that He has heard our prayer, and that he is doing what we asked him to do, but we just can't see the signs....but we need to see them because it's the signs that lead to miracles. Somebody who needs and wants a miracle, please help me teach this chapter. Make this decree:

GOD'S CURE TO THE CORONAVIRUS Chief Ambassador Dr. Vernard Johnson

36.
1. The enemy does not want me to receive my miracles.
2. But too late devil, I've already got the victory.
3. I see signs all around me that a miracle is coming.
4. And even before the miracle arrives, I'm going to,
5. Thank God for the signs.

Now take a few minutes to give God some praise just for the signs.

Yeah, yeah, just for the signs.......because if you don't recognize the signs, you may miss your miracle. I'm reminded of the popular story from Truthbook about the drowning man...most of you have already heard...but I want to remind you of it again because it will illustrate my point). There was a christian man who was caught in a flood, and the water kept rising. It flooded his house out so, until the man had to move to the floor upstairs. The water kept rising
until he had to go up in the attic. The water didn't stop rising....he climbed out of the attic window and got up on the roof, but the water kept rising. Then the man prayed, "Lord save me".....and God assured him that he would save him. All of a sudden somebody came by in:

1. A canoe.....but the man said no, the Lord said he was going to save me.
2. A motor boat...jump down into the water and swim over to our boat...the man said, "No, the Lord said he was going to save me.
3. A helicopter came by and dropped a rope.....the man said, "No, I can't take that rope because the Lord said he was going to save me.

   The water kept on rising and the man drowned. When he got to heaven, he asked God, "God, you told me that you were going to save me, why did you let me drown?"......and God said, "I sent a cannoe, a motor boat and a hellicopter for you, but you couldn't see my blessings....I sent all kinds of signs that I was trying to save you and give you a miracle, but you couldn't see the signs..................Open your eyes and see 'your' signs. Everything will be alright.

There is a story in the Bible, 2Kings 20 that illustrates our topic for this chapter.

The Principal Person:	Jehovah God
Minor Characters:	Hezekiah and Isaiah
Time Line:	This occurred around 636 BC
The Location	This took place in Israel around Jerusalem
The Historicity:	Reflects that Hezekiah, the king of Israel who followed his father Ahaz as king, he became sick unto death ......and God spoke to Isaiah the prophet and told him

37.
    to tell Hezekiah the king to set his house in order, because he was going to die and not recover from this sickness..........

After perusing this topic, perspicaciously looking at it more carefully, applying it to my life, and then extracting some meat from the topic that can be spiritual food for all of our souls, I began to see some principles about signs, that could change every one of our lives forever if we would only apply them. I want to share them with you:

1. **Whatever you do, don't forget to pray**.....prayer does change things....(2 Ki 20:2 KJV) Then he turned his face to the wall, and prayed unto the LORD,
2. **Sometimes it's alright to remind God**....(2 Ki 20:3 KJV) I beseech thee, O LORD,
3. remember now how I have walked before thee in truth and with a perfect heart, and have done that which is good in thy sight. And Hezekiah wept sore.
4. **Don't be ashamed to weep.** (2 Ki 20:5 KJV) B.....Thus saith the LORD, the God of David thy father, I have heard thy prayer, I have seen thy tears: behold, I will heal thee: on the third day thou shalt go up unto the house of the LORD.
(2 Ki 20:5 KJV) Turn again, and tell Hezekiah the captain of my people, Thus saith the LORD, the God of David thy father, I have heard thy prayer, I have seen thy tears: behold, I will heal thee: on the third day thou shalt go up unto the house of the LORD. (2 Ki 20:6 KJV) And I will add unto thy days fifteen years; and I will deliver thee and this city out of the hand of the king of Assyria; and I will defend this city for mine own sake, and for my servant David's sake.
[Now here is the main principal that I want you to see today.
5. **Take God at His word and thank God for the signs.** As I close today, may I say this to you........Somebody got sick with back problems, stomach problems, heart problems.....somebody got sick with cancer, diabetes problems, lung problems, and all kinds of problems....problems on your job, financial problems, problems with your bills, relationship problems, and God has sent all kinds of signs to you....over and over and over again that He heard your cry, and that He is healing you, but your eyes are closed3
6. to what God is doing and has already done for 'you'. You have not seen the sings. God says, "Open your eyes" and see the signs (I have already sent you a canoe, a motor boat, a hellicopter) but you haven't seen the signs....and when you see them, don't forget to thank God for the signs, because if you thank Him for what He has already done, it will move Him to do more.

I thank God for the signs.....and if we can only recognize the signs, and learn to praise God for them, I believe it will encourage God to do more for us. Let me give you a testimony. Elder

38.

Tyler is the Assistant of Amazing Grace Church....the church where I am the Pastor. Around two years ago, Elder Tyler became very ill. I'm getting so encouraged because I'm seeing signs that God is healing him:
1. He was almost dead...had a stroke and bleeding on the brain
2. They had to drain the blood off of his brain
3. This left him paralyzed on his left side......
4. He laid there like he was comotose......not moving anything.
5. A few days later, I began to see some signs......he began to move his right hand and right toes
6. A few days after that, he began to lift his hand above his head......signs......one day his 38. niece Geneva was going to brush his hair, and he took the brush out of her hand and brushed his own hair....a sign.
7. His progress of recovery has been slow, but there are so many signs take indicate he is getting better.

His recovery progress caused me to think about our President. Mr. President, how could it hurt our nation for Americans to think that we have 'A Man Of God' as our leader. I'm not referring to somebody who has gone off the deep end like a religious fanatic...but someone who is not ashamed to lead the people in prayer, and who shows that he honors and respects God. It's not enough to say a prayer in the privacy of your home, or in the Oval Office. America needs to hear and see a Godly leader too. This would be a sign that our country is on the right track toward being healed....and I know that this is not about politics, but I believe this would touch the hearts of the people and the people would vote for a man like that.

CHAPTER VIII
EXCELLENCE WITHOUT THE ANOINTING

I want to commend many of you reading this book right now. Many of you have the spirit of excellence. What a wonderful blessing.

    a. Whatever you do at your job, you do with the spirit of excellence…when they train you, you learn your job right away…..you make sure you do your assignment, and if anyone is lagging behind, you even act as a team player and 37.

    b. help others who are lagging behind complete their job

    c. Many of you are excellent educators…you dot every 'I' & cross every 't'

    d. Many of you are excellent cooks…you can't just burn…you can sho' nuff burn.

    e. Many of you keep you house in the spirit of excellence….it's so clean, people feel like they need to take their shoes over when they enter.

    f. Some of you keep you car with excellence…..it's always clean and shinny

    g. You keep the yard at your house with a spirit of excellent

    h. Dress with the spirit of excellence…hair and personal higene are always excellent.

And that's great! But I want to challenge you to go a step further. I not only want you to do things with excellence, but I want to challenge you to allow the anointing of God to take you to a new level. I hadn't given a lot of thought about the anointing in that way until I recently heard about an excellent beautician who 39.

is known for having anointed hands. I was in a restaurant getting a meal and I noticed an elderly lady who I could tell, must have just left the beauty shop. I could tell she was one of the saints, so I spoke and complemented her hair…She said "thank you" and then went on tell me that her beautician says she has anointed hands. I thought within myself….her beautician is not only one who strives for excellence in doing hair, but she' is a beautician who has anointed hands. Then I began to think, "I want that to be our approach at Amazing Grace, not for just a few, but for everyone….my prayer is for everyone to have excellence….with…..………the anointing.

I know we are all trying to keep a safe distance from others. I know that all of us are trying not to infect others. I know we all are trying to be very careful, and that is excellent; but I

40.

believe if we include GOD and His anointing in the equation, we would see a change.

If you know that the anointing gives you power, make this decree:

1. I know you have some hurts, some pains, and some problems in your life...these are yokes that need to be destroyed.
2. Money can't destroy the yokes, and education can't destroy the yokes.
3. So ask God for the anointing, because it's only the anointing that destroys the yoke.

And if you believe that, say, "Lord, I want the anointing", and then give God some praise.

1. The ushers and greeters greet people with excellence, but what if the ushers and greeters not only greeted people with excellence, but with the anointing?

38.

2. What if the choir sang every son with the anointing?
3. What if the offering was always received with the anointing?
4. What if people always read the scripture not only with excellence, but with the anointing?
5. What if people did the Inspirational Message with the anointing?
6. What if people gave their praise report with the anointing?
7. What if the announcements were given under the anointing?
8. What if even the welcome was given with the anointing?

I believe that every part of a church service should not only be done with excellence, but if people pray and consecrate themselves, I believe that every part of the service can be done with the anointing.

Why? Again, it is the anointing that destroys the yoke. When we look at Acts the 3rd chapter, we can see an example. So please allow me to peruse it, perspicaciously examine it, see how it can fit in my life, and then exact some meat from the chapter that shall be spiritual food for all our souls. In 3rd chapter of Acts, verse 6, it says, "Then Peter said, Silver and gold have I none; but such as I have give I thee: In the name of Jesus Christ of Nazareth rise up and walk." Peter is a disciple of Jesus and he's real picky about things.....he believes in doing things with excellence and by protocol. Let me prove this to you. When Jesus went to wash the feet of

Peter. Peter felt like it was improper and not protocol for his leader to wash his feet. In John 13:8, Peter said to (Jesus), "Thou shalt never wash my feet..." but Jesus answered him and said, "If I wash thee not, thou hast no part with me. Then in John 3:9, "Simon Peter saith unto him, Lord, not my feet only, but also my hands and my head." Praise the Lord. Peter said all of this in the flesh….he had not received the anointed of God. But later in Acts 2, it is recorded that the disciples were in the upper room on the Day of Pentecost ………..Peter was there and received the baptism of the Holy Ghost. Now, here in (Acts 3:2 KJV) it says, "And a certain man lame from his mother's womb was carried, whom they laid daily at the gate of the temple which is called Beautiful, to ask alms of them that entered into the temple;"

(Acts 3:3 KJV) says, "Who seeing Peter and John about to go into the temple asked an alms. (Acts 3:4 KJV) And Peter, fastening his eyes upon him with John, said, Look on us. (Acts 3:5 KJV) And he gave heed unto them, expecting to receive something of them. (Acts 3:6 KJV) Then Peter said, "Silver and gold have I none; but such as I have, give I thee: In the name of Jesus Christ of Nazareth rise up and walk." (Acts 3:7 tells us "And he took him by the right hand, and lifted him up: and immediately his feet and ankle bones received strength. (verse 8) And he leaping up stood, and walked, and entered with them into the temple, walking, and leaping, and praising God."

Now, I want you to see this. In the earlier life of Peter, he simply believed in doing things with excellence, but he didn't have the anointing. However the Word tells us that in:

Acts 2:1 (KJV) And when the day of Pentecost was fully come, they were all with one accord in one place. (Acts 2:2 KJV) And <u>suddenly</u> there came a <u>sound from heaven</u> <u>as of a rushing mighty wind</u>, and it <u>filled all the house</u> where they were sitting. (Acts 2:3 KJV) And there <u>appeared unto them cloven tongues like as of fire</u>, and it <u>sat upon each of them</u>. And verse 4 tells us that "…they were all filled with the Holy Ghost, and began to speak with other tongues, as the Spirit gave them utterance."

Peter was in that number and received the Holy Ghost too. So since Peter was already a man of excellence, he 40.

was now <u>a man of excellence with the anointing</u>. That's why the lame man received his healing. The anointing was present:

But what about people who are without the anointing:

1. They are like sounding brass, or a tinkling cymbal.
2. No anointing….no power
3. Little anointing…little power
4. A great anointing…great power

42.

You see in order to have the real anointing on your life, you must humble yourself and go to God with an attitude of 'nothing', Lord, I don't know nothing, I can't do nothing without you, I ain't nothing without you Lord, and I sho can't do nothing without you…I can't do nothing until you come. So Lord, have your way in my soul. When you get to that point, the anointing can take over and bring great miracles to your life. You see, that's what the older saints said….Lord, I can't do nothing until you come…..that's why they would sing those praise songs like "I'm a soldier in the army of the Lord", or "I wish somebody's soul would catch on fire, and burn with the Holy Ghost"….they were waiting on the power of God to fall on them….then, when the power of God would come, great and marvelous things would happen…people would get saved, healed, set free and delivered.

I thank God for education….degrees and talents, but most of all, I thank God for the anointing on my life. Why….There are 4 reasons why we all need the anointing…

1. **There are so many desperate people in this world today who need help.** Look at (Acts 3:2 KJV). And a certain man lame from his mother's womb was carried, whom they laid daily at the gate of the temple which is called Beautiful, to ask alms of them that entered into the temple." This man was desperate.
2. **People are looking to you for help**…
Acts 3:4 KJV) And Peter, fastening his eyes upon him with John, said, Look on us. (Acts 3:5 KJV) And he gave heed unto them, expecting to receive something of them.
3. **People need yokes destroyed**….and miracles to happen
What are yokes….problems that need to be solved…burdens that need to be lifted… oppression or bondage that someone is in, trouble that someone needs help on, a load or a weight that needs to be lifted. In the 3rd chapter of Acts, verse 6, it says, "Then Peter said, Silver and gold have I none; but such as I have give I thee: In the name of Jesus Christ of Nazareth rise up and walk." This was a yoke that needed to be destroyed…Acts 3:4 KJV) And Peter, fastening his eyes upon him with John, said, Look on us. (Acts 3:5 KJV) And he gave heed unto them, expecting to receive something of them, and instead of money, he received a miracle. Peter said, "In the name of Jesus Christ of Nazareth rise up and walk. (Acts 3:7 KJV) And he took him by the right hand, and lifted him up: and immediately his feet and ankle bones received strength. (Acts 3:8 KJV)
4. **People need to praise God**….Psalms 102:18 tells us that, "…God created people to paise the LORD." Here in Acts 3:8, it tells us that when the man got healed,

43.

> "And he leaping up stood, and walked, and entered with them into the temple, walking,
> and leaping, and praising God." (Acts 3:9 KJV) And all the people saw him walking and praising God:

To have the anointing, you must spend time with Jesus… (Acts 2:1 KJV) And when the day of Pentecost was fully come, they were all with one accord in one place. Did you know that the disciples were in the upper room for 50 days before the Holy Ghost fell. What were they doing all that time. They were spending time with Jesus. The Lord showed me that when you spend time with Him…4 things happen…1. Focus, ushers in, positions, encourages others:

CHAPTER IX
CRY FOUL

It had to be 2:45 when the LORD woke me up this morning and said for me to tell the people to 'cry foul'. God knows I didn't want to get up….I tried not to get up, but I knew that if I didn't get up I would lose what the Lord had for the people and me. God said, "If you are living for the Lord, you have a right to cry 'foul'!!!

The purpose of this chapter is to reawaken you to the rights you have as a child of the King. "God spoke to my mind in the Spirit Realm and He repeated it a couple of times,

"I cry foul, I cry foul?? Lord I don't know anything about "I CRY FOUL, I said!" Nevertheless, He kept on pushing that on me; and saying, "Son, it's time for the people of God to cry 'Foul'.

I didn't know what God was trying to get over to me, but then God reminded me of the

44.

playoff game I saw the other night. It was between (I believe) Texas Tech and Virginia. The game was tied and it was in the last few seconds of the game, that one of the key players on the Virginia Team took a shot at the basketball goal to win the game, but he missed. It looked like the game was over and there was no way that Virginia could win the game. But one of the key players on the other team (Texas Tech) touched the Virginia player while he was trying to make the shot and the referee blew the whistle and cried foul. Now the referee is the main official of the game who keeps the players from breaking the rules.....whatever he says, goes.

Even though the player on the Virginia team missed the shot, they stopped the game and allowed him to step to the free throw line to take a couple of free throws....free shots a shots without anybody trying to stop him because that's the rule of the game........the opponent can try to block your shot, but he is not suppose to touch you, and if he does, the rules say the shooter gets two or three free shots...depending on the play. Virginia won the game, but one of the main reasons why Virginia won the game is because of the foul.....the opponent from Texas Tech illegally touch the shooter. The rules said that he did not have permission to touch the shooter.

When God showed me that, I began to understood what God was trying to get over to me when He said in the Spirit realm, it's time, it's time, it's time for the people of God to cry foul. The enemy does not have permission to touch us, and if he does try to touch us, we should go to God and cry foul. I think you understand my point, but in this chapter I want to blow the whistle on the enemy and cry 'foul'. God made the Coronavirus, in fact, according to John 1:3, God made every thing, both good and evil. I am glad that God made the evil too, because if He had not made evil too, the enemy (the devil) would have tried to make it, and if the devil had made evil, he would have killed you 20 years ago. However, I believe that he tries to use everything that God created against God's people. I believe the enemy has used the Coronavirus to hurt and bring pain to people all over the world.

Despite this, Oh my God!!! It's time! I said, "It's time!!!" It's been time for the people of God not to sit back while the enemy tries to destroy our nation...tries to hurt us....tries to touch us..tries to attack us......we need to go to God (the referee and judge of all things) and cry FOUL!!!!!!!!! In almost every area of life, people are crying foul. In basketball,

football, soccer, in the court room and in many other situations people are crying FOUL!!!!

45.

Listen, the devil does not have a right to touch us. He must get permission from God...ask Job. Our knees have never bowed to Baal. We are the ones who wouldn't serve any other God....and as for me and my house, we will serve the Lord. And this morning, I have come to blow the whistle on the devil and cry "Foul". You mean to tell me, you can't look back over your shoulders and see all the times the enemy has tried to hinder you, to touch you and your family, and he didn't have permission. Didn't you recognize it. You better recognize it now and open your mouth and cry 'ffff', ffffff', fffffff', (somebody help me blow this whistle, and cry) ffffffffffooowll). You can win this game through crying unto the referee (who is GOD Jehoveh), Foul!!!!". Help me name some things that the enemy didn't have any business bringing on 'you'.....cause you are living for God and are God's child. As I close this chapter of this book, I want you to get ready to cry foul over every one of these things that the enemy is trying to bring on the people of GOD!!! All he is doing is trying to take your dominion from you. The Word says, you have a right to cry 'foul'!!! 'You' have dominion on this earth. If you are on the Lord's side, you have a right to cry 'foul'!!! Let's go to the basketball court and cry 'foul' on everything that the enemy is attacking the people of God with....and after every one of them, I want you to help me cry 'foul":

1. Brest cancer   cry foul!!!!!!
2. Throat cancer   cry foul!!!!!!
3. Cervical cancer   cry foul!!!!!!
4. Prostrate cancer   cry foul!!!!!!
5. Lung cancer   cry foul!!!!!!
6. Pancreatic cancer   cry foul!!!!!!
7. Brain cancer   cry foul!!!!!!
8. Liver cancer   cry foul!!!!!!
9. Bone cancer,   cry foul!!!!!!
10. Diabetes   cry foul!!!!!!
11. High blood   cry foul!!!!!!
12. Low blood   cry foul!!!!!!
13. Carpal Tunnel   cry foul!!!!!!
14. Strokes   cry foul!!!!!!
15. Heart attacks   cry foul!!!!!!
16. Asthma   cry foul!!!!!!
17. COPD Disease)   cry foul!!!!!!
18. Gout   cry foul!!!!!!
19. Dialysis   cry foul!!!!!!
20. Cataracks   cry foul!!!!!!
21. Gum Abscesses   cry foul!!!!!!

46.

22. Dizziness   cry foul!!!!!!
23. Inner Ear Infection cry foul!!!!!!
24. Sinus infections.   cry foul!!!!!!
25. Sinus drips...   cry foul!!!!!!
26. Constant Coughing   cry foul!!!!!!
27. Sore Throat   cry foul!!!!!!
28. Ulcers   cry foul!!!!!!
29. He-cups   cry foul!!!!!!
30. Panic Attacks   cry foul!!!!!!
31. Feelings of Fear   cry foul!!!!!!
32. Impatience   cry foul!!!!!!
33. Chronic Pain Attacks cry foul!!!!!!
34. Chronic Back Pains   cry foul!!!!!!
35. Chronic Arthritis Pains cry foul!!!!!!
36. Chronic Headaches   cry foul!!!!!!
37. Chronic Feet Pain   cry foul!!!!!!
38. Chronic Leg Pain   cry foul!!!!!!
39. Chronic Neck Pain   cry foul!!!!!!
40. Chronic Arm Pain   cry foul!!!!!!
41. Hip Pain & side pain cry foul!!!!!!
42. Chronic Stomach Pain cry foul!!!!!!
43. Chronic Knee Pain   cry foul!!!!!!
44. Chronic tiredness   cry foul!!!!!!
45. Joint Paint.. shoulders cry foul!!!!!!
46. Depression   cry foul!!!!!!
47. Side affects from drugs cry foul!!!!!!
48. Lupus   cry foul!!!!!!
49. Cycle Cell Anemia   cry foul!!!!!!
50. Occurring Boils   cry foul!!!!!!
51. Amputations   cry foul!!!!!!
52. Flu.....   cry foul!!!!!!
53. Pneumonia   cry foul!!!!!!
54. Kidney Problems   cry foul!!!!!!
55. Anxiety Attacks   cry foul!!!!!!
56. Crones Disease   cry foul!!!!!!
57. D'Andre Syndrome   cry foul!!!!!!
58. Blood Clots   cry foul!!!!!!
59. Mussel spasms   cry foul!!!!!!
60. Degenitive disk disease cry foul!!!!!!

1. Weakness...............the enemy doesn't want you to be strong & have control over that situation you've been going through, but the Word says in (Eph 6:10-11 KJV) Finally, my brethren, be strong in the Lord, and in the power of his might. Put on the whole armor of God, that ye may be able to stand against the wiles of the devil." Cry foul!!!!!!!!
2. The enemy is trying to have dictatorship over your life; but you better go to God and cry 'ffffffoul'!!!...........the enemy is trying to be a dictator over your life and try to tell you what he wants you to do, rather than what GOD wants you to do. Blow the whistle on him and cry 'foul!!!' You have the Word on your side. Jesus said in (Mark 3:35 KJV) <u>For whosoever shall do the will of God</u>, the same is my brother, and my sister, and my mother.
3. Confusion...............the enemy is trying to use witchcraft on you...trying to confuse your mind, but blow the whistle and cry foul, because (1 Cor 14:33 KJV) says, "For God is not the author of confusion, but of peace, as in all churches of the saints."
4. Disorder.................no peace....(1 Cor 14:33 KJV) For God is not the author of confusion, but of peace, as in all churches of the saints.
5. Mutiny...................dominion is not a take over spirit.....it is what the enemy tried to
6. do in heaven. Cry foul!!!!!!
7. Rebellion................a spirit that tells God 'no'....(1 Sam 15:23, "For rebellion is as the sin of witchcraft, and stubbornness is as iniquity and idolatry."
8. Revolt.....................the enemy trying to make you revolt against GOD's word
9. Riot.........................the enemy <u>fighting</u> in your mind. Cry foul!!!!!!
10. Revolution.............the enemy wanting you to fight against what God says
11. Servitude................the enemy wanting you to serve 'him', not God. cry foul!!!!!!
12. Inferiority..............Satan making you think you don't deserve what God gave
13. Insubordination....not obeying God. cry foul!!!!!!
14. Submission.............to the enemy, not God. Cry foul!!!!!!
15. Silly or stupidity....dominion is not silliness or stupidity, dominion centers around wisdom and knowledge. On the enemy, cry foul!!!!!!

CHAPTER X
AN UNCOMMON CHURCH

An uncommon church is one that will obey God. 2 Corinthians 6:16 (KJV) tells us, "And what agreement hath the temple of God with idols? for ye are the temple of the living God; as God hath said, I will dwell in them, and walk in them; and I will be their God, and they shall be my people." 2 Corinthians 6:17 (KJV) declares, "Wherefore come out from among them, and be ye separate, saith the Lord, and touch not the unclean thing; and I will receive you." Matthew 7:13 (KJV) says, "Enter ye in at the strait gate: for wide is the gate, and broad is the way, that leadeth to destruction, and many there be which go in thereat." 1 Peter 2:9 (KJV) says, "But ye are a chosen generation, a royal priesthood, an holy nation, a peculiar people; that ye should show forth the praises of him who hath called you out of darkness into his marvellous light:"

Matthew 7:14 (KJV) shares, "Because strait is the gate, and narrow is the way, which leadeth unto life, and few there be that find it." This chapter is titles "An Uncommon Church" because that is what God is looking for in this pandemic hour....an uncommon church. God is tired of these churches trying to be common with the world. The Bible says in Matthew 7:13 (KJV) "Enter ye in at the strait gate: for wide is the gate, and broad is the way, that leadeth to destruction," and many there be which go in thereat: You see, there are sooooo many people and churches that are compromising with the world......they are merging with with the world.....and merging is when you take two items and blend them together so well that you cannot tell one from the other.....merging with the world.

1. Their choirs are trying to sing like the world and move like the world. Example (some church musicals).
2. They are getting their ideas from the world.
3. They want to dress like the world
4. They want to talk like the world
5. They can tell you all about the world, but they can't tell you anything about Jesus.

People are not going to church any more to worship God. If they go, they are going for a show. 2 Timothy 4:3-4 (KJV) tells us, "For the time will come when they will not endure sound doctrine; but after their own lusts shall they heap to themselves teachers, having itching ears; 2 Timothy 4:4 (KJV) And they shall turn away their ears from the truth, and shall be turned unto fables." That time is NOW!

But God is looking for an uncommon church. Again, Matthew 7:14 (KJV) declares

49.

6. "Because strait is the gate, and narrow is the way, which leadeth unto life, and few there be that find it." Listen, whatever you do, don't take the broad way. That's the common way that many people in the world is trying to take, but the Bible says that it leads to destruction. A <u>common</u> church is one that is on the broad road. It is not concerned about what GOD wants. It is only concerned about what pleases the people. You see, most of the time the people want to take the broad road; but in order to have <u>an uncommon church</u>, we as men and women of God have to be uncommon ourselves, and stand for what GOD wants us to do.....we are living in the last days; and in the last days, the Good Book tells us in 2 Timothy 4:2 (KJV), "Preach the word; be instant in season, out of season; reprove, rebuke, exhort with all longsuffering and doctrine." Then it tells us in the next verse 3 "For the time will come when they will not endure sound doctrine; but after their own lusts shall they heap to themselves teachers, having itching ears." People only want to hear things that make them feel good. Verse 4 says, " And they shall turn away their ears from the truth, and shall be turned unto fables."

As I began to read more in 2 Timothy the 4th chapter, 3 principals seemed to jumped out at me concerning an uncommon church. First of all, an <u>uncommon</u> church are:

1. <u>People who want to hear from God and endure sound doctrine</u>. This is a day when many people don't want to hear and certainly don't want to endure sound doctrine. Now what is sound doctrine? It is teaching that helps people embrace the life and the beliefs of true Christianity....and Christianity is the doctrine that teaches people to live like Jesus Christ. You see, people don't want to live like Jesus. They want to live like the world.
2. <u>People who don't have itching ears</u>. You see, when people are itching they want to scratch that itch, and when they scratch the spot where they are itching, it makes them feel good. So people who have itching ears are people who just want to hear stuff that makes them feel good. But an uncommon church is made up of people who want to hear the truth. John 8:32 (KJV) "And ye shall know the truth, and the truth shall make you free. And John 8:36 (KJV) tells us, If the Son therefore shall make you free, ye shall be free indeed:"

    In an <u>uncommon</u> church people are those who are free from the itch. You see itching ears carry residue with it. It not only affects the ears, but it also affects other portions of your life. It will not only make people only want to hear stuff that makes them feel good, but watch it!!! If you are not careful, itching ears will cause people to become a church hopper. Watch...........it's like a prostitute....always walking the street looking for something new or <u>somebody</u> new.

50. And as I cross reference this, I see it's <u>the same spirit</u> that Satan exemplified in Job 2:1.....when the sons of God came to present themselves before the LORD, and Satan came also among them to present himself before the LORD. Job 2:2 (KJV) says, "And the LORD said unto Satan, From whence comest thou? And Satan answered the LORD, and said, From going to and fro in the earth, and from walking up and down in it (and may I add....like a prostitute....always looking for something or somebody. You see God is settled! He's "the same yesterday, today and forever more"............but the world is always looking for a thrill. Watch that.....watch becoming frillish or thrillish.

3. Uncommon church people <u>don't turn their ears away from the truth</u>. They love hearing the truth. They want to be helped. My deceased mother (Mother Adlee Johnson taught......"if you can't take it, you won't make it".....And Paul said in 1 Corinthians 15:58 (KJV) ". . . be ye stedfast, unmoveable, always abounding in the work of the Lord, forasmuch as ye know that your labour is not in vain in the Lord."
Please allow me to give you one more characteristic of an uncommon church.

Here's a bonus.....

4. <u>An uncommon church is one that wins lost souls to Christ.</u> People in this day and time don't seem to be concernd about lost souls anymore. They are only concerned about themselves and maybe their family. They seem to be always selfish, so lost souls is the last thing they think about. In Fort Worth, Texas, My ministry rented 46 convention centers, and I went across the county doing "Soul Winning Concerts." People go to concerts when they will not go to anything else. My team and I were able to win close to 12,000 lost souls to Christ. Many times souls that even look as though they will never, never be saved will come to Christ; but an uncommon church doesn't give up on them.

I asked some people how they would describe an un common church. Here is what they said. An uncommon church is one that:

1. Believes the word of God (Jeanette Murphy)
2. Preaches hope (Charla Gray)
3. Doesn't compromise or debate the gospel (Bro. Chris)
4. Teaches the importance of The Holy Ghost (Debra Johnson)
5. Displays Jesus Christ here on earth (Shelia Brown)
6. They are givers (Dr. Julie Hagan)
7. It has a leader who listens to the Spirit of God

51.

An uncommon church is one that tries to keep God's commandments. Below is a list of many of the things that an uncommon church strives to avoid...............sins..................

<u>108 SINS</u>

What is sin: an act, thought, or way of behaving that goes against the law or teachings of God. God is righteous and all disobedience (being out of the will of God) is sin. Below are 108 transgressions. The only person who never committed any of these transgressions was Jesus:
49.

1. Slothfulness—Hebrews 6:12 and Proverbs 19:15
2. Missing your blessings—living in a way you miss them: Deuteronomy 28:2-6
3. Backsliding—Jeremiah 3:14 and Hosea 14:4
4. High-mindedness—1 Timothy 6:17 and Rom 12:3
5. Usury—Nehemiah 5:7 and Exodus 22:25
6. Late for worship—Hebrews 6:11-12
7. Neglecting God—Exodus 20:3
8. Being too busy for God— Matthews 6:33
9. Placing other god's before Jehovah—Lev 19:4
10. Worshiping idol gods—Exodus 20:5 (NIV)
11. Being involved in cults—Deuteronomy 18:10 (NIV)
12. Not obeying God—Rom 6:16 and Josh 5:6
13. Not doing God's perfect will—Deuteronomy 7:11, 1 Sam 15:22
14. Enmity (hatred) against God—James 4:4
15. Haven't led anyone to Christ— Luke 14:23, Luke 19:10
16. Controlling your own life—Proverbs 3:6 and 2 Chronicles 30:8
17. Neglecting your family—1 Tim 5:8
18. Man—not being the spiritual leader of your household—1 Peter 2:5, Mat 10:38
19. Not obeying them that have rule over you—Hebrews 13:17
20. Not obeying your parents—Ephesians 6:1
21. Neglecting reading the Word of God—2 Timothy 2:15
22. Compromising God's Word—Psalms 119:101, Mat 5:18 and Psalms 119:105
23. Neglecting The Church— Psalms 133
24. Not paying your tithes—Mal 3:8-10
25. Teaching false doctrines—1 Tim 4:1 & 2 (NIV)
26. Giving false prophesy—1 John 4:3
27. Stirring up strife—Proverbs 15:18

52.

28. Going back to bondage—Gal 5:1
29. Grieving the Holy Spirit—Ephesians 4:30
30. Not treating those you hire right—Leviticus 19:13
31. Being a church hopper— James 1:8
32. Been a church whore—Gal 5:19
33. Been a church pimp—Proverbs 28:8 & Ephesians 4:22
34. Lusting after the women—1 John 2:16
35. Lusting after the men—1 John 2:16
36. Orgies— Galatians 5:19 (NIV)
37. Causing confusion in The Church—1 Corinthians 14:33 and Proverbs 6:19
38. Gossiping—Ephesians 4:29, Proverbs 20:19, Proverbs 16:28, Proverbs 15:2
    39. Not controlling your anger—Ephesians 4:31 Proverbs 16:32

40. Carrying grudges-bitter about something—James 5:9, 1 Peter 4:8-9, John 13:34
41. Un-forgiveness--haven't forgiven your brother or sister—Mat 18:35
42. Judging others—Mat 7:1 and Mat 7:2
43. Jealousy—Song 8:6 and Gal 5:19--21 (NIV)
44. A nasty attitude— Philippians 2:5 (NIV) and Ephesians 4:29
45. Stirring up discord—Galatians 5:19 and Proverbs 6:19
46. Hatred—Galatians 5:19
47. A false witness that speaks lies—Proverbs 6:16-19
48. Causing mischief—Proverbs 6:16-19
49. A wicked heart—Proverbs 8:7, Proverbs 6:16-19 (NIV)
50. Doing evil to your neighbor—Psalms 15:1-3, Rom 2:16-17
51. Devising wicked things—Proverbs 6:16-19
52. Prejudice—Proverbs 24:23, Romans 2:11, Proverbs 21:2
53. Looking down on others—Gal 5:26 (NIV)
    54. High-minded—1 Tim 6:17
55. Proud spirit—Psalms 101:5 and Proverbs 27:2
56. Mistreating the widows and orphans— Exodus 22:22 (NIV) and 1 Tim 5:3
57. Self righteous—Ezek 33:13
58. Selfish—James 3:16 (NIV)
59. A user of others—Proverbs 28:8
60. Generational sin—Acts 2:40 (NIV)
61. Murdering— Exodus 20:13 and Revelations 22:14-15
62. Witchcraft—Deuteronomy 18:10 and Exodus 22:18
63. Idolatry—Rev 22:14-15
64. Consulting Mediums—Psychic readings, horoscope readings and palm readings:

53.

Lev 20:6 (NIV), Deuteronomy 18:10 and Rev 22:14-15
65. Demon possession—Romans 6:12-13 and Mark 1:32
66. Blasphemy against the Holy Ghost—Mat 12:31-32
67. Suicide—to destroy God's property is a sin. Matthew 19:18, 1 Cor. 6:19
68. Smoking—to destroy God's property is a sin: 1 Corinthians 6:19
69. Drinking—to destroy God's property is a sin: 1 Corinthians 6:19, Proverbs 23:21, Galatians 5:19 (NIV)
70. Cursing—2 Tim 2:16 and Lev 18:21
71. Gambling—Proverbs 28:8
72. Drugs— to destroy God's property is a sin: 1 Corinthians 6:19
73. A glutton, with no self discipline—Proverbs 23:20 (NIV) and Proverbs 23:21
74. A Liar—Proverbs 6:16 and Rev 21:8
75. Cheating—Exodus 20:14, Eph 5:25
76. Stealing—Exodus 20:15
77. Sneaking—2 Tim 3:6
78. Backbiting—Lev 19:16 (NIV) and Psalms 15:1-3
79. Swearing—James 5:12
80. Fits of rage—Galatians 5:19
81. A persecutor of the saints—Mat 18:6, Acts 26:10 (NIV) 1 Corinthians 6:2,
82. Coveting your neighbor's husband or wife—Exodus 20:17
83. Fornication—Gal 5:19
84. Adultery—James 4:4, Galatians 5:19 and Matthew 5:28
85. Abortion—Exodus 20:13, Deuteronomy 27:25 and Proverbs 6:16 & 17
86. Rape—2 Sam 13:14 (NIV) and 2 Sam 13:32 (NIV)
87. A transvestite— 1 Corinthians 6:9 (NIV)
88. Having Sex with animals— Rev 21:8 (NIV) and Exodus 22:19
89. Child molestation—Rev 21:8 (NIV) and Matthew 18:5-6
90. Incest—Lev 18:6 (NIV), Matthew 18:5-6
91. Prostitution—Hosea 6:10 (NIV)
92. A whore monger—Rev 22:14-15
93. Sexually harassing—Proverbs 6:25 and 1 Corinthians 6:9 (NIV)
94. Pornography—1 John 2:16, Galatians 5:16, Col 3:5-6 (NIV)
95. Lasciviousness—sex acts in a lewd or vulgar way: Mark 7:21-22 & Gal 5:19
96. Homosexuality—1 Corinthians 6:9 (NIV) and Romans 1:27 (NIV)
97. Lesbianism—Romans 1:26 and 1 Corinthians 6:9 (NIV)
98. The sin of omission—Rev 3:3 (NIV); (1 John 3:24 NIV), and (Acts 5:29 KJV)
99. Atheism—Psalms 14:1
100. Backsliding— Jeremiah 3:14
101. A lover of money— 1 Tim 6:10 and Proverbs 11:28

102. Lover of worldliness—1 John 2:15 & 16; James 4:4
103. Speaking idle words—Mat 12:36
104. Unclean ess—Gal 5:19: Lev. 5:2 & 3; Lev. 7:21
105. Wrath (a rage of anger)—Gal 5:19
106. Emulation—Gal 5:20 (trying to be like the world)
107. Taking revenge—Romans 12:19 and Leviticus 19:18
108. No respect for the church—Leviticus 19:30 and Mark 11:17

CHAPTER XI

HOW TO GET ASTONISHING THINGS TO HAPPEN

The confession: God said that He wishes above all things that I would prosper and be in health, even my soul soul prospers. Today, I shall hear a Word that will help me prosper. I will not only be a hearer of the Word, but also a doer of the Word; and I shall go up up up up, up up up up, UP!!!!! In JESUS name I decree and declare this. Amen.
Now if you believe that give GOD a real shout!!!!

We need some astonishing things to happen here in America during this pandemic hour. I want to tell you about something astonishing that happened to Peter (the disciple of Jesus) and from what happened to him, I want us to establish some principles that we can extract from his story that will help us in our daily lives. Here is the true story.

(Mat 14:3-8- (KJV) "For Herod had laid hold on John, and bound him, and put him in prison for Herodias' sake, his brother Philip's wife. For John said unto him, It is not lawful for thee to have her. And when he would have put him to death, he feared the multitude, because they counted him as a prophet.

55.

But when Herod's birthday was kept, the daughter of Herodias danced before them, and pleased Herod. Whereupon he promised with an oath to give her whatsoever she would ask. And she, being before instructed of her mother, said, Give me here John Baptist's head in a charger. "

Then in Acts 12:1-7, it tells us, "Now about that time Herod the king stretched forth his hands to vex certain of the church. He had chopped off the head of John the Baptist and he killed James the brother of John with the sword.
And because he saw it pleased the Jews, he proceeded further to take Peter also. (Then were the days of unleavened bread.) And when he had apprehended him, he put him in prison, and delivered him to four quaternions of soldiers to keep him; intending after Easter to bring him forth to the people. Peter therefore was kept in prison: but prayer was made without ceasing of the church unto God for him. And when Herod would have brought him forth, the same night Peter was sleeping between two soldiers, bound with two chains: and the keepers before the door kept the prison. And, behold, the angel of the Lord came upon him, and a light shined in the prison: and he smote Peter on the side, and raised him up, saying, Arise up quickly. And his chains fell off from his hands. Here are the principles from this story that I want to share with you:

1. <u>Expect the enemy to come to vex the God's people...to vex you</u>............
   (Acts 12:1 KJV) Now about that time Herod the king stretched forth his hands to vex certain of the church. This Coronavirus is vexing our world.
   (Acts 12:2 KJV) And Herod killed James the brother of John with the sword.
   Acts 12:3 (KJV) And because he saw it pleased the Jews, he proceeded further to take Peter also. (Then were the days of unleavened bread.)
2. <u>Keep Praying</u>......(Acts 12:5 KJV) it's not over.......Peter therefore was kept in prison: but prayer was made without ceasing of the church unto God for him.
3. <u>Keep believing.....Expect God to do "exceeding abundantly above all you can ask or think"</u>.....(Acts 12:7 KJV) And, behold, the angel of the Lord came upon him, and a light shined in the prison: and he smote Peter on the side, and raised him up, saying, Arise up quickly. And his chains fell off from his hands. 57/

56.

\(Acts 12:8 KJV) And the angel said unto him, Gird thyself, and bind on thy sandals. And so he did. And he saith unto him, Cast thy garment about thee, and follow me. (Acts 12:9 KJV) And he went out, and followed him; and wist not that it was true which was done by the angel; but thought he saw a vision. (Acts 12:10 KJV) When they were past the first and the second ward, they came unto the iron gate that leadeth unto the city; which opened to them of his own accord: and they went out, and passed on through one street; and forthwith the angel departed from him.

(Acts 12:11 KJV) And when Peter was come to himself, he said, Now I know of a surety, that the Lord hath sent his angel, and hath delivered me out of the hand of Herod, and from all the expectation of the people of the Jews. (Acts 12:12 KJV) 54.

And when he had considered the thing, he came to the house of Mary the mother of John, whose surname was Mark; where many were gathered together praying. Acts 12:13 KJV) And as Peter knocked at the door of the gate, a damsel came to hearken, named Rhoda. (Acts 12:14 KJV) And when she knew Peter's voice, she opened not the gate for gladness, but ran in, and told how Peter stood before the gate. (Acts 12:15 KJV) And they said unto her, Thou art mad. But she constantly affirmed that it was even so. Then said they, It is his angel. (Acts 12:16 KJV) But Peter continued knocking: and when they had opened the door, and saw him, they were astonished.
4. Keep knocking on the door.....eventually, someone will hear you.
5. Keep telling your testimony.....be persistent....someone will listen to you.

CHAPTER XII
MUCH OBLIGED

When this pandemic is over, and even before it is over, everyone needs to say to God..........."Much Obliged!!!!!" 'Much obliged' means thank you. In fact, that is what everyone should be saying right now. I know it's bad, but it could be much, much worse. A gospel singing group called The William Brothers sang a song that helps us to know why. It is titled "Your Grace And Mercy", and the lyrics say, "Your grace and mercy brought me through. I'm living each moment because of you. I want to praise and thank you too. Cause your grace and mercy brought me through." That epitomizes a 'much oblige to GOD!

57.

I want to make a very important announcement. "You have the most loving and caring God that has ever been known to man." He knows every sin that you have ever committed in your life, and that you are committing now and every sin that you will commit in your future, and yet, He still loves you. He's there for you through the thick and the thin. He heals you when you are sick, encourages you when you are down....fights for you when you are attacked. He hasn't forgotten you even in this pandemic, but He wants to get our attention. The seniors say, "Jesus remembers when others forget". He's just the best........and I want to talk to those who realize this, and who really love God. God does not have many who really want to live for Him. The Bible says in (Mat 7:13-14 KJV) ".....wide is the gate, and broad is the way, that leadeth to destruction, and many there be which go in thereat; and narrow is the way, which leadeth unto life, and few there be that find it." Since God does not have many who are trying their best to live for Him, He rewards those who do. When you live for Him, it seems like out of nowhere, when you least thinking about it, GOD will drop a 'much oblige' on you, again, that means 'thank you'.....and may I tell you something? Just keep on doing good, because can't nobody thank you like God can thank you:

1. You can be sick dieing and the doctors can't find out what is wrong with you, and all of the sudden, God sends your Pastor or first Lady, or one of the saints to pray for you and God heals you. That's a much oblige.
2. You can have bad credit and need a car, and God makes the computer or the man say 'yes' when you know it should say 'no'. That's a much oblige.
3. You can be working on your job and not even be thinking about a promotion, and God can lay you on your bosses heart and give you a promotion making more money......that's a much oblige.
4. You can move here from out of town, and your wife can be on the way to join you, but you don't even have a house for you'all to live in, but out of no where God gives you a beautiful town home to live in.....that's a much oblige.
5. A bully might be messing with your child at school every day, and perhaps you don't know what to do....but you get down on your knees and pray about it, and out of no where that family with that bully son moves to another part of the city which takes him out of your son's school....that's a much oblige.
6. You can want a house and know you don't have the credit or the income to afford the house, but God.........God moves in your behalf and you don't even know how it happened, but you got the house........that's a much oblige.
7. Your house payment might be going up and God even changed your mortgage payment.......that's a 'much oblige'.
8. When GOD helped you keep your house when the devil was trying to take it..'NO'

I'm trying to tell you that sometimes out of nowhere, when you least expect it, when you live

GOD'S CURE TO THE CORONAVIRUS Chief Ambassador Dr. Vernard Johnson

5\8.

for the Lord, sometimes out of nowhere God will give you a 'much oblige'......:

1. Thank you for living for me
2. Thank you for honoring me
3. Thank you for not bowing your knees to idol gods
4. Thank you for suffering through the Coronavirus.
5. Thank you for not throwing in the towel.
6. Thank you for turning your faces toward me
7. I know many people in this day are raising their hands and bowing to basketball players, baseball players, football players and even to soccer players, but thank you because your hands are bowing to Me....the only true and living God.

Much oblige my son, 'much oblige' my daughter. Our chapter today gives us a stellar example 56.

of a group of people who received a much oblige from the Lord. Please allow me to tell you about it, and then I will close this chapter of this book. It is found in 2Chronicles 20:17.

Principal Person	Jehovah God
Minor Persons:	Jehoshaphat and the Children of Israel, the Moabites, the Ammonites, and other tribes.
Time Line:	This happened around 856 BC....which points out that God had the back of His people 856 years before Christ was born. What should that mean to 'you'. It says if God had their backs then, He has 'our' backs now during this Pandemic.
Location:	Judah in Jerusalem
The Historicity:	Reflects in (2 Chr 20:1 KJV) It came to pass after this also, that the children of Moab, and the children of Ammon, and with them other beside the Ammonites, came against Jehoshaphat to battle.....they be in Hazazontamar, which is Engedi. And the Bible tells us in the 20th chapter and the 3rd verse, that Jehoshaphat feared, and set himself to seek the LORD, and proclaimed a fast throughout all Judah.................

Now there are some golden nuggets in this chapter that will help you get a 'much oblige'. Jehoshaphat and the people of God received a 'much oblige' from God. What are the golden nuggets we can learn from him so that we can receive a 'much oblige' from God too? In the

59.

Spirit realm, I can hear Jehoshaphat saying, to receive a 'much oblige' from God, first of all:

1. **Don't be afraid to fear**.....if that's what it takes to get you to honor God and keep His commandments, then don't be afraid to fear. I know the Word tells us in (2 Tim 1:7 56. KJV) "For God hath not given us the spirit of fear; but of power, and of love, and of a sound mind;" but that's a different kind of fear. It just like words that can have two different connotations. They can mean one thing in one situation, but mean another thing in another situation. When the Word says, "For God did not give us the spirit of fear," That's talking about the fear of the devil and evil. God does not want you to have that, but there is a good kind of fear. It is the fear of God. It is the fear that helps you live right....that helps you keep God's commandments. (Psa 34:9 KJV) says, "O fear the LORD, ye his saints: for there is no want to them that fear him;" and (Psa 103:17 KJV) tells us, "But the mercy of the LORD is from everlasting to everlasting upon them that fear him." Jehoshaphat feared, and set himself to seek the LORD.........

   It's just like some of the nieces and nephews who don't want to be saved. The Bible says in (Eccl 7:3 KJV) Sorrow is better than laughter: for by the sadness of the countenance the heart is made better. They may be laughing now doing what they want to do and living any kind of way, because their mama is alive, their sister is alive, their baby is alive, but God can use sorrow to make them fear Him, but it's all to make them better. Not only is Jehoshaphat saying through this chapter, 1. Don't be afraid to fear, if that's what it takes to move you to seek God, but secondly, Jehoshaphat tells us go: **Fast:** (2 Chr 20:3 KJV) says, Jehoshaphat ".....proclaimed a fast throughout all Judah." Listen, miracles can come from fasting.............'My testimony'.

   Not only is Jehoshaphat saying through this chapter, 1. Don't be afraid to fear, if that's what it takes to move you to seek God; and not only is he urging us to fast to get a 'much oblige', but thirdly Jehoshaphat tells us to:
2. **Remind God of His promises**......"(2 Chr 20:5 KJV) And Jehoshaphat stood in the congregation of Judah and Jerusalem, in the house of the LORD, before the new court, and said, O LORD God of our fathers, art not thou God in heaven? and rulest not thou over all the kingdoms of the heathen? and in thine hand is there not power and might, so that none is able to withstand thee? He's reminding GOD of His promise. Art not thou our God, who didst drive out the inhabitants of this land before thy people Israel, and gavest it to the seed of Abraham thy friend for ever? And they dwelt therein, and have built thee a sanctuary therein for thy name, saying, If, when evil cometh upon us, as the sword, judgment, or pestilence, or famine, we stand before this house, and in thy presence, (for thy name is in this house,) and cry unto thee in our affliction, then thou

60.

wilt hear and help. Verse 10, Jehoshaphat said, "And now, behold, the children of Ammon and Moab and mount Seir, whom thou wouldest not let Israel invade, when they came out of the land of Egypt, but they turned from them, and destroyed them not;

3. behold, I say, how they reward us, to come to cast us out of thy possession, which thou hast given us to inherit. Verse 12 he said, "O our God, wilt thou not judge them? for we have no might against this great company that cometh against us; neither know we what to do: but our eyes are upon thee. And verse 13 says, "And all Judah stood before the LORD, with their little ones, their wives, and their children."

Listen, has GOD made you any promises??? Remind God of what He promised you:

1. God you promised that you would supply my every need according to your riches in heaven.
2. God you promised that you wanted me to prosper even as my soul prospers.
3. God you promised that if your people, which are called by your name......
4. God you promised in Psalms 103:3, "that you are the God who would forgive all my iniquities; who who would heal all my diseases;
5. God you promised that you would be my protector.
6. God said that He was going to make many millionaires here at Amazing Grace, and almost every Sunday, I repeat it. I'm reminding God of His promise.

Listen, keep His promises before Him. He will do it....He will bring it to pass. God told Balaam in (Num 23:19 KJV) "God is not a man, that he should lie; neither the son of man, that he should repent: hath he said, and shall he not do it? or hath he spoken, and shall he not make it good?" He will keep His promises!!!!

Scripture Promises:
   a. (2 Cor 4:8 KJV) We are troubled on every side, yet not distressed; we are perplexed, but not in despair;

   b. (2 Cor 4:9 KJV) Persecuted, but not forsaken; cast down, but not destroyed;

   c. (2 Cor 4:10 KJV) Always bearing about in the body the dying of the Lord Jesus, that the life also of Jesus might be made manifest in our body.

God promised: That He would never leave us nor forsake us. He said, "And lo, I am with you even to the end of the world. Then He told us in (2 Cor 5:1 KJV) .....if our

61.

earthly house of this tabernacle were dissolved, we have a building of God, an house not made with hands, eternal in the heavens.

Just "...**lift up your eyes unto the hills**, from whence cometh your help. Your help cometh from the LORD, which made heaven and earth."

And **just believe** "...**on Jesus, as the scripture hath said**, out of your belly shall flow rivers of living water.

And then, **"In all thy ways acknowledge him**, and he shall direct thy paths."

And, **"Delight thyself also in the LORD**; and he shall give thee the desires of your heart." If we need help, we can "Look to the hills.....................our help comes from the LORD!

If enemies come against us, "No weapon formed................"

Then He promised, "The Lord is my light and my salvation...whom shall I fear."
(Psa 46:1 KJV) God is our refuge and strength, a very present help in trouble.
(Psa 91:1 KJV) He that dwelleth in the secret place of the most High shall abide under the shadow of the Almighty.
(Psa 27:1 KJV)The LORD is the strength of my life; of whom shall I be afraid?
Listen there are so many things that God has done for us, and we have failed to give Him a 'much oblige' for them. Why don't you stop right now and give it to Him?

CHAPTER XIII

YOU CANNOT DIE ON GOD'S ASSIGNMENT

Please make this confession: God said that He wishes above all things that I would prosper and be in health, even my soul soul prospers. Today, I shall read a Word that will help me prosper. I will not only be a reader of the Word, but also a doer of the Word; and I shall go up up up up, up up up up, UP!!!!! In JESUS name I decree and declare this. Amen. Now if you believe that give GOD a real shout!!!!

62.

(Jonah 2:10 KJV) And the LORD spake unto the fish, and it vomited out Jonah upon the dry land. (Jonah 3:1 KJV) And the word of the LORD came unto Jonah the second time, saying, (Jonah 3:2 KJV) ….take your assignment son……Arise, go unto Nineveh, that great city, and preach unto it the preaching that I bid thee.

How many of you reading this book want to live and not die???? I want to give you a secret about living. If you want to live and not die, I plead with you! Please, please, don't. allow the enemy to distract you today, and please don't allow the enemy to maneuver you into closing your ears again today. Hosea 4:6 tells us that "My people are destroyed for lack of knowledge: because thou hast rejected knowledge, I will also reject thee, that thou shalt be no priest to me: seeing thou hast forgotten the law of thy God, I will also forget thy children." Listen, blocking your ears from the truth not only affects 'you', but it will hurt your child too. That spirit of stubbornness and rebelliousness will not only dominate your life, but it will also start dominating your son, your daughter, and even the lives of your grandchildren too. Not only will you die a premature death, but they will too, and it all comes from a spirit of stubbornness and rebelliousness. Do

you remember that a few days ago God showed me the in time strategy that the enemy is trying to use on the saints……..he's trying to wear the saints out…..Why? He wants to get you out of the way….to kill you. Why? You are a threat to his kingdom. He knows you will either now or later, do damage to his kingdom…..and he knows if he can make you stubborn and rebellious, you probably will be too stubborn to accept your assignemt….then he can try to kill you.

But I'm getting ready to give you one of the keys to living and not dying. I hope you receive it…..here it is……..If you want to live and not die, then accept the assignment that GOD has sent to you; because you cannot die while on the assignment that God puts you on. My subject today is "You Cannot Die While On God's Assignment and my purpose is to prove this to you today, and then I want to help everyone recognize the assignment that God has sent or is sending to you.

As I begin today would you help me get this message over to somebody around you by making this decree. Tell somebody these words….say this out loud:

1. God does not want you to die a premature death.
2. He wants you to live and declare the works of the Lord.
3. And if you want to live and not die,
4. Then don't be stubborn and don't be rebellious, accept the assignment sent by

63.

5. GOD to you, and start doing the assignment, then you shall live and not die.

If you receive that, give God some praise!!!!

And before I get deep into the chapter, please allow me to say this, many of you who already have an assignment. The enemy is trying to get you off of your assignment. Why? He knows while you are on the assignment sent by God.....the assignment that God put you on, you cannot die.....so that means the enemy is trying his best to maneuver you off of that assignment....why, so he can try to kill you before your time. ....and that is.

also the reason why the enemy is trying to wear you down.....and the enemy is sending people to try to wear you down to get you away from your assignment. He doesn't even have respect for family members....the enemy will try to even use family members....your son, daughter, grandchildren, or anyone close <u>to you to get you off of your assignment</u>. He doesn't care who he uses. All he wants is for you to get away from your assignment to gain permission for him to try to kill you. When the battle becomes a little overwhelming for you, just remember that the battle is not yours anyway....the battle is the Lord's.

Now, I could prove my topic to you today, "You cannot die on God's assignment" by using:

1. Moses stood before the Pharaoh at least 10 times. The Pharaoh wanted to kill Moses but could not, because Moses was sent by God to do an assignment.
2. Elijah......it's not going to rain until I say so...the king searched for him to kill him.
3. Elisha......a whole army surrounded his house and could not kill him......he said to his servant "They that be with us are more than they that be with them."
4. The dry bones in the valley....some of the Israelites had been in a war....and their enemies had left them for dead, but some time later, God sends Ezekiel to speak to the dry bones. Folks, they had not finished their assignment, and what the devil
61
.
5. meant for evil, God meant it for their good.
6. Jonah.....but let me prove to you 'that you cannot die when you have an assignment sent by by God' by exegeting the chapter here in Jonah........there are at least 5 times in this chapter that Jonah could have died, but he didn't....he even prayed to die, but he couldn't. Let me try to show this to you. *****Read the

GOD'S CURE TO THE CORONAVIRUS   **Chief Ambassador Dr. Vernard Johnson**

Bible and deal with the story (Jonah 1).

64.

Now, when we first start reading the book of Jonah I see a problem. What is the problem? I see a stubborn, rebellious, arrogant and even crazy person......and I am wondering where all this is coming from. Then I realized that for Jonah to be this way, it had to come from somewhere else....so I began to study his background. Now, when you research his background, we find that Jonah was the son of Amittai. Who was Amittai and where did he come from. Amittia was from Gathhepher. Gathhepher was one of the chief cities of the Philistines. I immediately knew that the Philistines were the people who were against Jehovah God and the people of God. You remember when David (a man after God's on heart) went out to fight Goliath. Goliath was the soldier, and the king of the Philistines sent him out to represent them against the Israelliets in the valley of Elah. Goliath was a giant around 9 feet tall, so these people were from the Anakim seed (Philistine giants), and because they were giants, they were arrogant, stubborn and rebellious people....they had the attitude, can't nothing touch me, and can't nobody tell . me nothing. They were not on the Lord's side, they were on the enemy's side. Whatever you do, don't become stubborn and rebellious. You don't want to end up like Goliath....dead with his head cut off and wrapped up in a cloth and kept as a trophy.

Then I realized something else. God already knew about Jonah's background. God knows everything....but He still gave Jonah an assignment (pause). Can't you see....can't you see???? As stubborn, as rebellious, and as crazy as Jonah was, God still gave Jonah an assignment. Why??? To save.....his......life. , the enemy would have killed Jonah way before his time, but he couldn't. Why? Because he was on an assignment given to him by God. There are a whole lot of us who would have been dead a long time ago, but thank God, the devil couldn't kill you because you were on assignment sent by God.

You see, Jonah came from a background of stubborn and a rebellious seed. His father was stubborn and rebellious....couldn't help it. Those were his people, and because his father was stubborn and rebellious, it caused his son (Jonah) to be stubborn and rebellious....it was a generational curse. I'm trying my best to show you that sometimes the devil is not after 'you', he's after your child, or your grandchild....and you cannot afford to lose the battle and be that way, for your child's sake. Satan wants your child to be stubborn and rebellious because of what he has planned in your child's future. The Word says in 1Samuel 15:23, "For rebellion is as the sin of witchcraft. Can't you see? This witch is after your child.

But thank you Jesus, even though Jonah was stubborn and rebellious, he could not die....why? Because God had called him to do an assignement. He tried to go contrary to God's plan, but he could not get away from the assignment of God. Your child may be stubborn and rebellious right now, but I pray and hope that God has an assignment on his life. Just leave him in the hands of the Lord, and don't worry...because the enemy cannot kill him, because he can't die on God's assignment.

Please, please, take the assignment. God is trying to save your life. You remember Rayhab who hid the spies from Israel in her house. She told them, I know you are going to take the city, but remember me and my family. God spared her life because she recognized what God was doing, and she took the assignment. It saved her life. Please, please, get busy becoming a Prayer Ambassador, praying for all parts of the world. Many of you have been assigned to be:

1. In the choir....but you haven't taken the assignment, or you have become slowful with your assignment.

2. As one of the leaders of Amazing Grace, but you haven't taken your assiganment seriously, or you've been slothful with your assignment.

3. Ushers, greeters, deacons, leaders among the youth, mothers, hospitality workers, members to help build, and please don't become complacent on your assignment..

4. Preachers, missionaries, encouragers, but you have allowed the enemy to make you complacent on your assignment.

Get up and start working on your assignment again and you shall be bountifully blessed......the enemy wants you to stop your assignment, because he knows you cannot die on your assignment. But work your assignment. You may not see the blessings right now, but they are coming. Just keep the faith and keep working, and the blessings will come to pass

(Jonah 3:3 KJV) So Jonah arose, and went unto Nineveh, according to the word of the LORD. Now Nineveh was an exceeding great city of three days' journey.
(Jonah 3:4 KJV) And Jonah began to enter into the city a day's journey....
Jonah was angry and prayed to die, but could not. (Jonah 4:3 KJV) Therefore now, O LORD, take, I beseech thee, my life from me; for it is better for me to die than to live.

(Jonah 4:8 KJV) And it came to pass, when the sun did arise, that God prepared a vehement east wind; and the sun beat upon the head of Jonah, <u>that he fainted, and wished in himself to die, and said, It is better for me to die than to live.</u>

66.

But Jonah could not die. Why? Because the assignment which looked as though it was completed, was not completed. 'Jonah' was part of the assignment. God had to mold and shape Jonah into what He wanted him to be. He still had the wrong attitude......an arrogant attitude. It was all about him rather than God's people and God's assignment. He was ranting and raving about how he looked when God didn't do what he said. The people repented, but God had to get him straight.

In the last verse of Jonah, God said, "(Jonah 4:11 NIV) But Nineveh has more than a hundred and twenty thousand people who cannot tell their right hand from their left, and many cattle as well. <u>Should I not be concerned about that great city</u>?"

God is so ultra awesome. Some time ago, GOD spoke to my mind and heart and he told me to make Ambassadors. I said "What kind of Ambassadors, Lord.....and God said Prayer Ambassadors. I want you to get prayer all over the world. I didn't know why at the time, but I know why now. We started making FirstFruits Ambassadors. Many of the FirstFruit Ambassadors, Ambassadors Elect and Honorary Ambassadors are taking assignments to pray for a country and the world. We have just begun but we already have over 200 countries, states and territories combined; and with social media (Face Book, Instagram, Twitter, Youtube, LinkedIn, and numerous radio stations, the Network reports that FirstFruit Prayer Line now has over 1.7 billion listeners plus their families. What a marvelous journey we are on. Praise the LORD!!!!!! We are touching the world for Christ. Below are some of our Prayer Ambassadors and the assignments they have taken:

FIRSTFRUITS PRAYER AMBASSADORS
(Countries assigned to Ambassadors)

A few years ago, THE LORD said to me, "Son, I want you to make Ambassadors. I said, "Lord, what kind of Ambassadors," because I didn't understand. God said, "Prayer Ambassadors" who will pray for nations. I want you to get prayer all over the world." Not knowing what shape the world would be in, I just simply told God 'yes' Lord, and I started doing what God said do. I've been trying my best to get prayer all over the entire world. We now have over 200 nations, territories and other areas that have joined us; and with our international audience, we now have over 1.7 billion listeners plus their families. This journey doing the LORD'S work touching the world for Christ is absolutely incredible! Below are some examples of Ambassadors who are praying:

67.
1. America   Prayer Amb. To The United States.....Dr. Betty Joyce Johnson
2. Ber,ida   Prayer Amb. To Bermuda.........Dr. Betty Joyce Johnson
3. Israel   Prayer Amb. To Israel...............Freddie Cullins
4. Haiti   Prayer Amb. To Haiti...............Mo. Linda Farkye
5. Russia   Prayer Amb. To Nigeria & Russia.....Shelia Brown
6. Jamaica   Prayer Amb. To Jamaica & Peru.....Lucille Angelo
7. Bahamas & Iran   Prayer Amb. To The Bahamas & Iran...Barbara Gildersleeve
8. Nigeria & Russia   Prayer Amb. To Nigeria & Russia........Shelia Brown
9. So. Af. & Greece   Prayer Amb. To So. Africa & Greece, Ervon Coleman
10. South America   Prayer Amb. To S. America....Mo. Thelma Rush
11. West Africa   Prayer Amb. To West Africa...Joyce Long
12. Mexico   Prayer Amb. To Mexico.....Sharla Gray
13. S. E. Asia   Prayer Amb. To S. E. Asia, England, Jeanette Murphy
14. S. E.Asia   Prayer Amb. To Indonesia...............Jeanette Murphy
15. N. Japan   Prayer Amb. To N. Japan....Dr. Julie Hagan
16. South Japan   Prayer Amb. To South Japan & India, Mo. Earnestine Riley
17. Hawaii   Prayer Amb. To Hawaii and Isreal....Pastor Willie Johnson
18. UK   Prayer Amb. To UK....Mo. Rose Woods
19. Iraq   Prayer Amb. To Iraq.....Bernita Frierson
20. Costa Rica   Prayer Amb. To Costa Rica..... Pastor Leola James Jones
21. Canada   Prayer Amb.   Canada................Debra Johnson
22. Ireland   Prayer Amb. To Ireland.....Rosemary Dancer
23. Germany   Prayer Amb. To Germany....Dr. Kim Kennedy
24. China   Prayer Amb. To China.....Lady Christine Guy
25. Palestine   Prayer Amb. To Palestine.....Cotell Johnson
26. Barbados   Prayer Amb. To Barbados....Mo. Gladys Peterson
27. Italy   Prayer Amb. To Italy.....Debra Pryor
28. Guatemala   Prayer Amb. To Guatemala......Debra Johnson
29. Canada   Prayer Amb. To Canada....Apostle Willie Mae Adams
30. E Africa   Prayer Amb. To E. Africa. Latanya Williams.
31. Venezuela   Prayer Amb. To Venezuela.......Bro. Chris Johnson
32. New Zealand   Prayer Amb. To New Zealand......Min. Ronnie Richardson
33. Venezuela Min.   Prayer Amb. To Venezuela......Min. Chris Johnson
34. Brazil   Prayer Amb. To Brazil......Bro. Louis Brown
35. So. North Korea   Prayer Amb. To N & S Korea plus Spain......Teresa Stills
36. Portugal—   Prayer Amb. To Portugal......Carolyn Alexander
37. France   Prayer Amb. To France & Trenadad.....Wazene Cobb
38. Granada   Prayer Amb. To Granada.........Debra Johnson
39. Syria   Prayer Amb. To Syria...............Willie Mae Bush
40. China   Prayer Amb.   China...................Lady Christine Guy

68.

    41. Port a Rico   Prayer Amb. To Porta Rico...Mo. Jerlene Garnett

These territories and countries and numerous others are open for Prayer Ambassadors who will pray for countries:

- France
- Italy
- Bermuda
- England
- Scotland
- Iceland
- New Mexico
- Po ta Rico
- Pora Viaca
- Brazil
- Baru
- Ecuador
- Finland
- Guyana
- Indonesia
- Malaysia
- Mongolia
- Nigeria
- Nicaragua
- Pakistani
- Portugal
- Trinidad
- Ukraine

Taiwan and many, many others. If you are a Prayer Warrior and you would like to be assigned a country to pray for as a Prayer Ambassador; call (913) 406 4845

Take the assignment that GOD is calling you to..........to pray for a country........it may save your life; because you cannot die on God's assignment!!!

Chief Ambassador Dr. Vernard Johnson   GOD'S CURE TO THE CORONAVIRUS

CHAPTER XIV
A HUGE BLESSING, IS ON THE WAY TO YOUR HOUSE!!!

The confession: Say this to yourself, and if possible, say it out loud. God said that He wishes above all things that I would prosper and be in health, even my soul prospers.

Today, I shall read a Word that will help me prosper. I will not only be a reader of the Word, but also a doer of the Word; and I shall go up up up up, up up up up, UP!!!!! In JESUS name I decree and declare this. Amen. Now if you believe that....don't be embarrassed, give GOD a real shout!!!!

Child of God, I have seen the signs that a huge blessing is on the way to 'your house'. The enemy only takes time to attack when he sees a huge blessing is coming your way. Let me say that again. The enemy only takes time to attack when he sees that a huge blessing is on the way. Otherwise, he doesn't waist his time. He's in this battle to win, and he picks and chooses the battles that he will fight. Some of the little small things that people are experiencing, they think the enemy is doing....but the truth is, if the enemy wants to win this battle over this planet called earth, the enemy doesn't evem have time to do that, but when the cncmy sees a huge blessing on the way to 'you'....to you....to your house, that's when he takes time to attack.

Please say these words out loud or to yourself:

  1. It's been rough and it's been tough.
  2. But I must stay in the race even though I go through test,
  3. Because the more I go through
  3. I realize that it's just a sign,
  4. That a huge blessing is on the way to my house.

Now if you believe that, give God a shout!!!!!

It's proven throughout the Word of God. Every time people went through horrific attacks from the enemy, it was a true sign that a huge blessing was on the way:

  1. Esther.....all the Jews were being threatened with their lives, but it was a sign that

70.
   a huge blessing was on the way. God turned it around and all the Jews ended up being tremendously blessed and saved, but Hagan (the Agagite) instead of of Mordecai ended up hanging from the gallows.

2. Moses....was in a basket on the Nile River. It looked as though he would never be nothing, but a huge blessing was on the way. After the Children of Israel had suffered for over 440 years, Moses ended up being the deliverer of the Children of Israel.

3. Joseph......was put in a pit by his brothers. He went through test after test, but a huge blessing was on the way.....he ended up going from the pit to the palace, becoming a multi-millionaire, and becoming second in command over all of Egypt.

4. Job.....was the wealthiest man in the land, but through a test, God allowed the enemy to take everything that he had. His wife even told him to curse God and die, but it was a sign that a huge blessing was on the way. He ended up having double for his trouble. Job 42:12 (KJV) says, "So the LORD blessed the latter end of Job more than his beginning: for he had fourteen thousand sheep, and six thousand camels, and a thousand yoke of oxen, and a thousand she asses...also, he also had seven sons and three daughters...double for his trouble.

5. Jesus went through test after test after test, but it was because a huge blessing was on the way................He came through 42 generations and was born on earth to a virgin called Mary.
   a. Herod tried to kill him
   b. The Phrisees tried to destroy Him.
   c. They got jealous of Him and lied on him,
   d. They marched him from judgment hall to judgment hall.
   e. They condemned Him to die....but it was a sign that a huge blessing was on the way.
   f. They took Him to Calvary, stretched Him wide and dropped him low...He died on Friday, but it was a sign that a huge blessing was on the way, because on Sunday morning, He got up and became our love, joy hope, peace, our leader, our guide, our JESUS, our God, our rock, sword, shield...............and our reredeemer...............and He ended up as 'the messiah of the whole wide world.'

Please listen to me, the enemy brings all these attacks when he sees a huge blessing is on the way to your house. Is there anyone reading this book who has been going through attacks??? Hold on and don't faint, even though the enemy is trying to wear you down, because it's a true sign that a huge blessing must be on the way to your house.
It's like a huge tornado. You have to keep on going. You can't turn around because you

71.

will have to go right back through the same tornado. But if you keep on going, there is a huge blessing right in front of you....there is a light at the end of the storm.

We have a convention almost every other year, and I have noticed that every time the Convention is coming up, the enemy will do all kinds of attacks on us to try to stop it, but it's a true sign that a HUGE blessing is on the way. It's like rain. Some people say they feel a change in their body when it's about to rain, but may I say this, it may be a sure sign that a huge blessing is on the way to a land that needs to be watered. O children of God, through this pandemic, I sense that a huge blessing is on the way to our homes. What we are experiencing now is definitely a crisis. All I'm trying to tell you that it's a sign that a huge blessing is on the way to your house.

When the Lord was dealing with me to have a Convention, I thought about calling it a Conference, but the Lord impressed on my heart to call it a Convention. Many times a Convention is larger than a conference. The Lord sees the future. Could that be a sign that the Lord saw our future and was trying to tell us that by calling it a convention, a bigger blessing was on the way to our house??? Time will tell.

My wife (Dr. Betty) just called me on the phone at 5:40am....so I thought. I said, "You will be calling me back in a few minutes (she normally calls me at 5:45am to remind me to get on the Prayer Line). When I said, "You will be calling me back in a few minutes, there was silence on the phone for a minute, then she alerted me that it was not 6:40 in the morning, it was 6:40 in the evening....LOL! Wow! I then realized that I have been working too hard on finishing this book that I didn't even notice it was night instead of morning (LOL); but nevertheless, it may be a sure sign that a HUGE blessing is on the way to our house.

The Lord impress on my heart that the National Headquarters for our Convention would be in Kansas.....and each Ambassador would have a Conference in their own area. One of the nights during their conference would be to help the local Ambassador in that area, and one of the nights would be for the International Ambassador.....to help him finance all his work. It may be kind of rough right now, but I believe that in the future, a huge blessing will be coming to our Ambassadors and to the Chief Ambassador.

God showed me to encouraged you, so may I say this to you, "Oh people of God throughout the world, "Be encouraged!........be encouraged!!.........be encouraged!!! Be encouraged!!........be encouraged!!.........be encouraged!!!........be encouraged!........be encouraged!!........be encouraged!!!........be encouraged!!!........be encouraged!!........be encouraged!!!.......be encouraged!!!........be encouraged!!.........be encouraged!!!!!!!!"

CHAPTER XV
IRON SHARPENS IRON

One of the most urgent epidemics that is happening all around the world is the shortage of men. During this dispensation and epidemic here in America and around the world, the enemy is trying to annihilate men in every city......especially black men. If you will go to the courts you will begin to realize this even more. The courts are filled with 75% to 80% black and brown men. What's up with that????? It's an epidemic...all across the land.

And we as black men need to open our eyes and begin to see that there is an attack that has been launched against black and brown men...and this attack is coming from the enemy himself. The Apostle Paul said in Ephesians 6:12 (KJV) "For we wrestle not against flesh and blood, but against principalities, against powers, against the rulers of the darkness of this world, against spiritual wickedness in high places." O people of God, it's the enemy that is attacking the men. John on the Isle of Patmos describes the enemy so well that we will know who our attacker truly is. In Revelation 12:9 (KJV) John describes him. It says, "And the great dragon was cast out, that old serpent, called the Devil, and Satan, which deceiveth the whole world. That's why we have men who are confused.....confused about:

1. Gender.....they are being deceived by the one who comes to deceive the whole
2. world. Some men don't know whether they want to be a man or a woman.
3. Their role in the family. Some men take pride in only being 'a baby daddy'
4. Their role in the church. Some men are threatened by the church.

Just confused!; but "God is not the author of confusion, but of peace." God wants the men to be real men....in fact, when I looked at 2 Chronicles 17:13-16, I began to see that Godwants men to become mighty men of valour.....and that's what I want to talk about in this chapter....."Mighty Men Of Valour". Notice, in the Old Testament, we have several references of war, and when the kings of the Old Testament went to war, they depended on real men, and they called them "Mighty Men Of Valour". I began to look into this prehensile perception of men in this chapter, and I began to see some qualities and some principles that men should adopt for their lives, and if they do, it would help better their lives forever. So let's take a look at these principles of these 'Mighty Men Of

73.

Valor' in 2 Chronicles 17:13-16. First of all I noticed that they were leaders.

1. Look at 2 Chronicles 17:13-16: When we talk about iron sharpening iron, first of all we must have:
   a. A hard surface. You cannot sharpen iron with jelly-back men. They must be real men. And let me tell you what 'real men' are not.
      1. They are not just baby making machines. That is a lie that has been perpetrated by men on the street. Somebody lied and said, "You ain't no real man until you have made a baby," and many young men have bought that lie and they have messed up their lives.

      Example:
      I was getting my tire fixed at a tire place, and a young man around 18 was in the waiting room with me. I started to make conversation with him, and during the conversation he shared with me that he not only had a girlfriend, but he had several girlfriends, and they already had 7 babies for him. I could not believe my ears. I immediately knew that it was a trick by the enemy to completely destroy his life. To doom you to a life of poverty:

      a. What about the child support those mothers would need one day?
      b. One day every one of those children would need their father.
      c. What about parents day at school. Suppose two or three schools would have 'Parents Day' on the exact same day as one of the other children?
      d. Without a father in their life, what if those children would get in trouble with the law. Even if the father could be there, how far could his money go????
      2. And a 'real man' is not a 'male chauvinist pig'.......trying to dominate the woman and the entire family. "I'm the man!!!"

      Listen men, the devil is down here on earth attacking every person he possibly can.....and I have come to tell you that one of our main focuses should be on the men. Why men? Why has the enemy focused on 'men'?

      Because the enemy knows that the strength of a nation is still measured by the strength of the men. Strong men make a strong nation. Yes, we in America have strong women who are even in the Army, Navy, Marines, and in all armed forces, but let's admit that the real strength of our fighting forces are men.

74.

      a. It's the men who are physically strong. That's why it's a crime for a man to beat up on a woman.....because he is the stronger vessel.

      b. In 1 Corinthians 11:3 (KJV), God spoke to Paul who said, "But I would have you know, that the head of every man is Christ; and the head of the woman is the man; and the head of Christ is God. God, in his infinite wisdom arranged so that woman and her children would have some protection.

3. What is a man? In Psalms 8:4 (KJV) as David was marveling in the excellence of the glory of GOD, David said this, "What is man, that thou art mindful of him? and the son of man, that thou visitest him? (Psalms 8:5 (KJV) declares, "For thou hast made him a little lower than the angels, and hast crowned him with glory andhonor. Verse 6 says, "Thou madest him to have dominion over the works of thy hands; thou hast put all things under his feet:"

Genesis 1:26 (KJV) tells us, "And God said, Let us make man in our image, after our likeness: and let them have dominion over the fish of the sea, and over the foul of the air, and over the cattle, and over all the earth, and over every creeping thing that creepeth upon the earth." The next verse says, "So

God created man in his own image, in the image of God created he him; <u>male and female created</u> he them." Then in verse 28 it proclaims, "And God blessed them, and God said unto them, Be fruitful, and multiply, and replenish the earth, and subdue it: and have dominion over the fish of the sea, and over thefoul of the air, the cattle and over every creeping thing that creepeth upon the earth; and over every living thing that moveth upon the earth." (Galatians 3:28 (KJV) declares, "There is neither Jew nor Greek, there is neither bond nor free, there is <u>neither male nor female: for ye are all one in Christ Jesus."</u> so this chapter goes out to not only the men, but the women too.

Iron sharpens iron. We as men have to learn to:
1. Pray for each other
2. Encourage each other.
3. Support each other
4. Look out for each other
5. Sometimes call each other
6. G o to court for each other
7. Give money to each other

8. Help each other
9. Give a ride to each other
10. Intercede for each other
11. Be happy for each other
12. Share Godly tips with each other
13. Read the Bible with each other
14. Play sports with each other
15. Have faith for each other
16. Have meekness with each other
17. Have love for each other
18. Be joyful and be glad (when God blesses) for each other
19. Have peace with each other
20. Have gentleness toward each other
21. Have longsuffering toward each other
22. Have goodness toward each other against such there is no law.
23. Discourage each other against adultery, fornication, uncleanness, lasciviousness,
24. Discourage each other against idolatry, witchcraft, hatred, variance, emulations, wrath, strife, seditions, and heresies,
25. Discourage each other against envyings, murders, drunkenness, and revellings

CHAPTER XVI
SPEAK TO YOUR SINEWS

The confession: God said that He wishes above all things that I would prosper and be in health, even my soul prospers. Today, I shall hear a Word that will help me prosper. I will not only be a hearer of the Word, but also a doer of the Word; and I shall go up up up up, up up up up, UP!!!!! In JESUS name I decree it. Amen. Now if you believe that give GOD a real shout!!!!

Sinews are a type of tough tissue like tendons that connects muscle to the bone. The purpose of this message is to get help to those persons who are having pains in your joints and bones...even cancer in your bones, or any other disease in your bones. Even your loved ones. Hosea 4:6 tells us, "My people are destroyed for lack of knowledge:

because thou hast rejected knowledge, I will also reject thee, that thou shalt be no priest to me: seeing thou hast forgotten the law of thy God, I will also forget thy children."

If the doctor has said that something is affecting your bones in any way. I want to show you scripturally that if you are on an assignment for God, 'you' have the power to speak to your bones and joints to cause them to line up with the Word of God and be healed

In Ezekiel 34 God speaks to the prophet Ezekiel and tells him to prophesy "against the shepherds of Israel, prophesy, and say unto them, Thus saith the Lord GOD unto the shepherds; Woe be to the shepherds of Israel that do feed themselves! should not the shepherds feed the flocks? (Ezek 34:3 KJV) says, "Ye eat the fat, and ye clothe you with the wool, ye kill them that are fed: but ye feed not the flock. (Ezek 34:4 KJV) The diseased have ye not strengthened, neither have ye healed that which was sick, neither have ye bound up that which was broken, neither have ye brought again that which was driven away, neither have ye sought that which was lost; but with force and with cruelty have ye ruled them."

In Ezekiel 35 God tells Ezekiel to prophesy against Mt. Seir. Ezekiel 35:1 (KJV) says, "Moreover the word of the LORD came unto me, saying,

"(Ezek 35:2 KJV) Son of man, set thy face against mount Seir, and prophesy against it. (Ezek 35:3 KJV) And say unto it, Thus saith the Lord GOD; Behold, O mount Seir, I am against thee, and I will stretch out mine hand against thee, and I will make thee most desolate. (Ezek 35:4 KJV) I will lay thy cities waste, and thou shalt be desolate, and thou shalt know that I am the LORD. (Ezek 35:5 KJV) Because thou hast had a perpetual hatred, and hast shed the blood of the children of Israel by the force of the sword in the time of their calamity, in the time that their iniquity had an end: (Ezek 35:6 KJV) Therefore, as I live, saith the Lord GOD, I will prepare thee unto blood, and blood shall pursue thee: sith thou hast not hated blood, even blood shall pursue thee. (Ezek 35:7 KJV) Thus will I make mount Seir most desolate, and cut off from it him that passeth out and him that returneth."

In Ezekiel 36, God tells Ezekiel to prophesy unto the mountains of Israel, and say, "Ye mountains of Israel, hear the word of the LORD:"
(Ezek 36:2 KJV) "Thus saith the Lord GOD; Because the enemy hath said against you, Aha, even the ancient high places are ours in possession:"

(Ezek 36:3 KJV) "Therefore prophesy and say, Thus saith the Lord GOD; Because they have made you desolate, and swallowed you up on every side, that ye might be a

77.

possession unto the residue of the heathen, and ye are taken up in the lips of talkers, and are an infamy of the people:"

(Ezek 36:4 KJV) "Therefore, ye mountains of Israel, hear the word of the Lord GOD; Thus saith the Lord GOD to the mountains, and to the hills, to the rivers, and to the valleys, to the desolate wastes, and to the cities that are forsaken, which became a prey and derision to the residue of the heathen that are round about;"

(Ezek 36:5 KJV) "Therefore thus saith the Lord GOD; Surely in the fire of my jealousy have I spoken against the residue of the heathen, and against all Idumea, which have appointed my land into their possession with the joy of all their heart, with despiteful minds, to cast it out for a prey."

(Ezek 36:6 KJV) "Prophesy therefore concerning the land of Israel, and say unto the mountains, and to the hills, to the rivers, and to the valleys, Thus saith the Lord GOD; Behold, I have spoken in my jealousy and in my fury, because ye have borne the shame of the heathen:"

(Ezek 36:7-9 (KJV) "Therefore thus saith the Lord GOD; I have lifted up mine hand, Surely the heathen that are about you, they shall bear their shame. But ye, O mountains of Israel, ye shall shoot forth your branches, and yield your fruit to my people of Israel; for they are at hand to come. For, behold, I am for you, and I will turn unto you, and ye shall be tilled and sown:"

Now, in Ezekiel 37, it tells us, "

(Ezek 37:1 KJV) The hand of the LORD was upon me, and carried me out in the spirit of the LORD, and set me down in the midst of the valley which was full of bones,

(Ezek 37:2 KJV) And caused me to pass by them round about: and, behold, there were very many in the open valley; and, lo, they were very dry.

(Ezek 37:3 KJV) And he said unto me, Son of man, can these bones live? And I answered, O Lord GOD, thou knowest.

(Ezek 37:4 KJV) Again he said unto me, Prophesy upon these bones, and say unto them, O ye dry bones, hear the word of the LORD.

(Ezek 37:5 KJV) Thus saith the Lord GOD unto these bones; Behold, I will cause breath to enter into you, and ye shall live:

(Ezek 37:6-12 (KJV) And I will lay sinews upon you, and will bring up flesh upon you, and cover you with skin, and put breath in you, and ye shall live; and ye shall know that I am the LORD.

(Ezek 37:7 KJV) "So I prophesied as I was commanded: and as I prophesied, there was a noise, and behold a shaking, and the bones came together, bone to his bone."

(Ezek 37:8 KJV) "And when I beheld, lo, the sinews and the flesh came up upon them, and the skin covered them above: but there was no breath in them."

(Ezek 37:9 KJV) "Then said he unto me, Prophesy unto the wind, prophesy, son of man, and say to the wind, Thus saith the Lord GOD; Come from the four winds, O breath, and breathe upon these slain, that they may live."

(Ezek 37:10 KJV) "So I prophesied as he commanded me, and the breath came into them, and they lived, and stood up upon their feet, an exceeding great army."

(Ezek 37:11 KJV) "Then he said unto me, Son of man, these bones are the whole house of Israel: behold, they say, Our bones are dried, and our hope is lost: we are cut off for our parts."

(Ezek 37:12 KJV) "Therefore prophesy and say unto them, Thus saith the Lord GOD;

Behold, O my people, I will open your graves, and cause you to come up out of your graves, and bring you into the land of Israel."

(Mat 16:19 KJV) "And I will give unto thee the keys of the kingdom of heaven: and whatsoever thou shalt bind on earth shall be bound in heaven: and whatsoever thou shalt loose on earth shall be loosed in heaven."

In chapter 35 God commands Ezekiel to speak to Mt. Seir....a group of people who had fought against his people (animate objects)....with life.

In Chapter 36 God commanded Ezekiel to speak to the mountains that were being controlled by the enemies of God's people......mountains are inanimate objects. This illustrates that God is over animate and inanimate things.

79.

But in chapter 37, God speaks to Ezekiel and commands him to prophesy to inanimate objects and command them to become animate (objects with life...he commands bones to become animate....he is commanded to prophesy to lifeless objects and command them to live.)

Again I remind you of sinues: a piece of tough and strong fibrous collagen tissue attaching muscle to bones and bone to bone; a tendon or ligament.....tendons so tough and fibrous that they connect the muscle to bones. Hebrews 4:12 (KJV) says, "For the word of God is quick, and powerful, and sharper than any twoedged sword, piercing even to the dividing asunder of soul and spirit, and of the joints and marrow, and is a discerner of the thoughts and intents of the heart.

Now, who is Ezekiel........a man of God.....someone who is on assignment.....and may I say this, when you are on spiritual assignment you are sent by God, and the gates of hell shall not prevail against you. (Mat 16:18 KJV) "And I say also unto thee, That thou art Peter, and upon this rock I will build my church; and the gates of hell shall not prevail against it."

Mat 16:19 (KJV) tells us, "And I will give unto thee the keys of the kingdom of heaven: and whatsoever thou shalt bind on earth shall be bound in heaven: and whatsoever thou shalt loose on earth shall be loosed in heaven." Speak, speak, speak to your sinews!!!

CHAPTER XVII
DON'T ALLOW THE ENEMY TO WEAR YOU OUT

The enemy is trying to wear out anybody who is trying to do any good work to help people.......and Mr. President, the enemy is trying to wear you out.

The confession: God said that He wishes above all things that I would prosper and be in health, even my soul soul prospers. Today, I shall read a Word that will help me prosper. I will not only be a reader of the Word, but also a doer of the Word; and I shall go up up up up, up up up up, UP!!!!! In JESUS name I decree and declare this. Amen.
Now if you believe that and you are not ashamed, give GOD a real shout!!!!

Daniel 7:25 (KJV) says, " And he (meaning the enemy) shall speak great words against the most High, and shall <u>wear out</u> the saints of the most High, and think to change times and laws: and they shall be given into his hand until a time and times and the dividing of time."

(Mark 8:11-12 (NIV) declares, "The Pharisees came and began to question Jesus. To test him, they asked him for a sign from heaven. Verse 12 (NIV) says He (Jesus) sighed deeply (they were trying to wear Him out) and said, "Why does this generation ask for a miraculous sign? I tell you the truth, no sign will be given to it."

And then in (Mark 8:21 NIV) "He said to them, "Do you still not understand?" Jesus wasn't talking down to His disciples, He was just concerned about them...wanting them to understand.

This chapter is so very, very interesting, because it shares with the people of God and others the tactful strategy that the enemy is trying to use to work on the saints.....and he's trying to do this unaware....he's trying to be slick. I hope you hear me, because again, Hosea 4:6 says, "....my people are destroyed from lack of knowledge. "Because you have rejected knowledge, I also reject you as my priests; because you have ignored the law of your God, I also will ignore your children. "

81.

So I hope you receive this that the LORD is sending. The enemy is trying to wear out the saints. Daniel 7:25 tells us, "....and he (the enemy) shall <u>wear out</u> the saints of the most High. If you will look in Mark 8:111-21, satan (the devil) tried to use this same strategy on Jesus. He used the Pharaseas and Jesus' own disciples to try to work on wearing out Jesus. Look at what it says:

(Mark 8:12-21 (NIV) "...the Pharisees came asking Jesus for a miraculous sign.....and He (Jesus) sighed deeply and said, "Why does this generation ask for a miraculous sign? I tell you the truth, no sign will be given to it."

(Mark 8:13 NIV) "Then he left them, got back into the boat and crossed to the other side."

(Mark 8:14 NIV) "The disciples had forgotten to bring bread, except for 'one loaf' they had with them in the boat. They had forgotten that they just witnessed Jesus feeding 5,00 people besides the women and children with two fish and five loves of bread. "

Then He said in Mark 8:15 (NIV) "Be careful," Jesus warned them. "Watch out for the yeast of the Pharisees and that of Herod." The enemy (the devil) was trying to wear Him out.

(Mark 8:16 NIV) "They discussed this with one another and said, "It is because we have no bread." Ha, ha, ha!!! Silly disciples!!!!

(Mark 8:17 NIV) Aware of their discussion, Jesus asked them: "Why are you talking about having no bread? Do you still not see or understand? Are your hearts hardened?

Then the Lord said in Mark 8:18-21 (NIV) "Do you have eyes but fail to see, and ears but fail to hear? And don't you remember? Verse 19, "When I broke the five loaves for the five thousand, how many basketful of pieces did you pick up?" "Twelve," they replied."

(Mark 8:20 NIV) "And when I broke the seven loaves for the four thousand, how many basketfuls of pieces did you pick up?" They answered, "Seven."

(Mark 8:21 NIV) He said to them, "Do you still not understand?" Satan was using the disciples to try to wear Jesus out.

82.

Our chapter in Daniel....Daniel partially corresponds to the chapter in Revelation 12:3 ....., and it answers questions that have been plaguing people for centuries. In Revelation 12:3 which says, "And there appeared another wonder in heaven; and behold a great red dragon, having seven heads and ten horns, and seven crowns upon his heads." The question is frequently asked, what do the seven heads, the ten horns and the seven crowns represent? Hear in Daniel 7:24, the prophet Daniel answers this question. It says, "And the ten horns out of this kingdom are ten kings that shall arise".

You see, Daniel had a dream where he saw four beast coming up out of the sea....he describes three of the beast. The first was like a lion that had eagles wings and a heart like a man, the second like a bear that had 3 ribs in it's mouth, the 3rd was like a leopard that had 4 wings and 4 heads, and a 4th beast was the most dreadful of all. It had iron teeth, and 10 horns, and it had eyes. <u>But what really caught my attention was verse 25 which is about the 4th beast, which says</u>, (Dan 7:25 KJV) "And he shall speak great words against the most High, and shall <u>wear out</u> the saints of the most High."

In our chapter today, it demonstrates that Jesus left heaven with a goal, and that was to do what His father had sent Him to do. The purpose was to save the world that He, His Father and the Holy Ghost had made. He came through 42 generations to do it....and after He came to the world, He began to have so much success, the enemy (the devil) started trying to destroy Him. He tried to kill Him when He was a baby, and he kept trying to destroy Jesus at every age of His life. Finally, when He saw that he could not destroy Jesus or stop Him, the enemy started using the tactic of trying to wear Jesus down.

That's the same tactic that he is trying to use on God's people in this day and time. He knows that he can't get God's people to drink all night....he knows that he can't get the people of God to shoot up drugs....he knows that he can't get the saints to cuss folks out (most of us), so he uses the strategy of trying to wear the saints down. Before I close this chapter in my book, I want to get you who are reading this book to help people to understand this message even more. You must get it in your heart first. Would you open your mouth and make this decree after me....say these words:

1. I see now! The enemy has been trying to wear me down.
2. Trying to get me to not pray as much, fast as much, and not to have faith in God as much
3. But in the name of Jesus, I'm determined to pray more, fast more and believe God even more.
4. Cause in the name of JESUS, I'm NOT, going to let the devil, wear me down.

83.

Now if you really mean that, **open your mouth and give God a victory shout!!!**

The purpose of this chapter is truly to get you to open your eyes and see that the enemy is trying his best to wear you out. He's trying. I said "He's trying". That's his strategy in this day and time...to try to wear you down. That's why he gave you the 2 words, "I'm tired". He knows that whatever you loose on earth, will get in your spirit and cause you to become just that, because the Bible says if you loose it on earth, it will be loosed in heaven. Child of God, the enemy (the devil) is trying to wear you down and out.

After perusing the topic "Don't Let The Enemy Wear You Out", looking at it more carefully, applying it to my life, **and then extracting some meat from the topic that can be spiritual food for all of our souls, I began to see some principles concerning this topic that could change all of our lives. I want to share them with you.**

There are 3 principles that implores you to never allow the enemy to wear you down, and if you will take these principles and apply them to your life, I believe they will change your life forever. The chapter tells us, don't allow the enemy to wear you down because:

1. Your child's life depends on it. So the enemy will try to wear you out through your children.....and sometimes, it's not about 'you'. The enemy is trying to wear you down because He's after your child or children....The enemy knows that it's 'you' who is standing in the way of him destroying your child; and if he wears you down, when you stop praying for your child, when 'you' stop pleading the resurrection blood of Jesus over
your child, he can sift your child as wheat and destroy them; but somebody who sees what the enemy is trying to do, ought to declare, "Not on my watch, devil."

> Example...some people know that I like to watch the animal channel, and on that channel, I saw a lion trying to watch and wait on an opportunity to attack a baby gorilla. The lion was trying to wear (the silverback) the adult gorilla down. Although the female gorilla conceived the baby gorilla, it was the male gorilla'sresponsibility to protect the baby gorilla. The lion thought the baby was unprotected, and when the lion thought he had worn the male gorilla down, he made his approach, but as soon as he started to head toward the baby gorilla, the silverback went to the baby gorilla and just looked at the lion, as if to say, "NO NO lion, not on my watch. You shall not kill my baby. I will fight you with everything in me".......and guess what.....the lion backed off.

Listen mamas and dads reading this book, you got to become like a silverback .....Take the anointed on your life and fight the enemy, and say, "NO NO devil, not on my watch. You cannot have my child." I will fight you with everything in my being. NO NO!!!!

The enemy will back off. But don't leave the back door opened and think the enemy won't try to come in the back door.....he will try again and again to wear you down....but you can't let him wear you down.....your son's, daughter's, grandchild's, grandson's life is at stake. If you let the enemy get your child, (your son, your daughter) that means that lion will then try to kill your grandchild too. I'm not trying to scare you. I'm trying to prepare you. You cannot allow the enemy to wear you down.

And Pastors and first ladies, you cannot allow the enemy to wear you down. 'You' are the target, because the enemy believes that if he can wear you down, then he thinks he can destroy the church; don't let him wear you down or out!

2. **'Your' future depends on it**.....so the enemy is trying to wear you out because he doesn't want you to have eternal life....because whether you go to heaven or hell may be determined from whether or not you allow the enemy to wear you down.
3. The future of the world depends on you.....so the enemy is trying to wear out people all over the world with this Coronavirus. 'You' have been called to help win this war on he world, not to lose it......and that is why the enemy is trying to wear you out. The world is in trouble. If you as a believer in God, allow the enemy to wear you down, down ......wear the people of God down....the world might be lost. God is depending on 'you'. Jesus said to His disciples in (Luke 10:2 KJV) "........"The harvest truly is great, but the laborers are few: pray ye therefore the Lord of the harvest, that he would send forth laborers into his harvest.

Listen God's people, we must not fail. If 'we' God's people would humble ourselves....get on our knees and pray; and seek His face; and turn from our wicked ways, then would God hear from heaven (the Son and the Holy Spirit) would agree as one, and He would forgive our sins and heal the land.....he would drive this Coronavirus completely out of the land. God made it......He made the evil and the good; and since He made it, He can order it to leave. Amen!

85. Example: We have a man on our Prayer Line named Chris Johnson. We call him Minister Chris. His passion is winning lost souls to Christ. He has won hundreds....perhaps even thousands of lost souls to Christ; but why do you think that God has him on our Prayer Line around The Chief Ambassador (as I am called, Dr. Vernard Johnson) God wants him to hear and watch me come on this Prayer Line, day after day, after day because God wants to demonstrate to him that He doesn't want him to allow the devil to wear him down. He is on the wall, but God doesn't want him to come down....in fact, all of us ought to get on that wall and start going to the highway and hedges compelling men, women, boys and girls to come to Jesus. Those who are doing that, please don't allow the enemy to wear you down. It's crucial. Your child's life depends on it, your future depends on it, and the future of the world is depending on it.

GOD needs some men of valor, and some women of valor....who will stand up to the enemy and say:

1. I see now! Enemy, you have been trying to wear me out.
2. To get me to stop praying as much, stop fasting as much, and to not have faith in God as much.
3. But in the name of Jesus, devil, you are a liar!!!!!!!! I'm determined to pray more, fast more and believe God even more.
4. Because in the name of JESUS, I'm NOT, going to let you, devil, wear me down or out. I realize now even more than ever before, that I am, more than a conqueror.......and I will win all my wars if I don't quit.

CHAPTER XVIII
TURN IT OVER TO JESUS

(Mat 6:31 KJV) Therefore take no thought, saying, What shall we eat? or, What shall we drink? or, Wherewithal shall we be clothed?

The confession: God said that He wishes above all things that I would prosper and be in health, even my soul soul prospers. Today, I shall read a Word that will help me prosper. I will not only be a reader of the Word, but also a doer of the Word; and I shall go up up up up, up up up up, UP!!!!! In JESUS name I decree and declare this. Amen.

86.

Now again, if you believe that and you are not ashamed, give GOD a real shout!!!!

The Lord has me to write this chapter to help all of us. God wants all of us to stop worrying about our problems. Matthew 6:28-30 (KJV) tells us, "And why take ye thought for raiment? Consider the lilies of the field, how they grow; they toil not, neither do they spin: and yet I say unto you, That even Solomon in all his glory was not arrayed like one of these. Verse 30 says, "Wherefore, if God so clothe the grass of the field, which to day is, and to morrow is cast into the oven, shall he not much more clothe you, O ye of little faith?

1. I know you have some problems that have been bothering you
2. But may I help you?
3. Don't worry about it.
4. God already knows about it
5. And Jesus will help you, if you turn it over to Him.

In this chapter, I want to talk about "Turn It Over To Jesus". Yes, yes, that's what we all need to do.....turn it over to Jesus. We cannot handle the Coronavirus or this pandemic; and when things are too big for us to handle, turn it over to Jesus.

Now, that's easy to say, but it's a little more difficult to do, because we are so accustomed to handling things ourselves. We don't enjoy depending on anyone. I looked at the royal wedding between Prince Harry and Meghan Markle on yesterday, and I saw in their marriage a great example of what I am referring to in this chapter. Meghan 'had' to do that. It was quite evident that Meghan was the main person that planned her wedding.......for it was <u>non-traditional</u>...totally against what any royal planner from England would have done.....a black gospel choir...a sermon from a black preacher..... with the queen of England squirming in her seat while it was going on. I'm sure that Meghan thought it out very carefully....and knowing how the enemy does, I'm sure he tried to get her to worry; but she didn't look worried. She looked calm. It is quite evident that she prayed and turned everything over to God. I don't know if she has heard the gospel song or the lyrics that say, "Jesus will work it out, if you let Him.....turn it over to Jesus"....but that's exactly what it appears that she did....she turned it over to Jesus and He worked it out. All over the world, they were talking about how beautiful the wedding was.

In our chapter, we see a greater faith than that of Meghan's. God spoke to Abraham and told him in, Genesis 22:2-3 (NIV) "Take your son, your only son, Isaac, whom you love, and go to the region of Moriah. Sacrifice him there as a burnt offering.

87.

mountains I will tell you about." Verse 3 says, "Early the next morning Abraham got up and saddled his donkey. He took with him two of his servants and his son Isaac. " Now, Abraham trusted God so much, when he had cut enough wood for the burnt offering, he set out for the place God had told him about. Genesis 22:4 (NIV) tells us, "On the third day Abraham looked up and saw the place in the distance. What he was doing was extremely difficult, but he didn't worry about it, because he turned it over to God. When he arrived at the place of sacrifice and raised the knife up in the air to slay his son, An angel shouted from heaven, "ABRAHAM!!!!! Stay your hand" He looked over to the side and God had a ram in the bushes waiting to replace his son as the sacrifice.

Wow!!!!!! The Lord sent me today to remind you in this book to "Turn It Over To Jesus". The Lord can work it out for you. While you are trying to figure it out, God has already worked it out. This pandemic and COVID 19 is too much for us, so we must turn it over to Jesus. Many times, God allows some things to come on you to push you into your destiny, but God knows about it. Just trust the anointing and give the anointing time to work. God may use 'you', or He may use someone else, but He will fix the problem for you.

Thank God, He led me to raise the money to buy our building; and we paid it off the first day we moved in....other wise I don't know how we would make it through this pandemic. However, our BPU utility bills have been extremely high. What do I do??? I simply keep the faith, keep working and turn it over to Jesus.

A few of the shingles came off our church roof due to strong storms. What did I do??? I turned it over to Jesus.

Listen, whatever your problem may be, if you can't handle it, turn it over to Jesus. The Word says in Matthew 6:28-29 (KJV) "And why take ye thought for raiment? Consider the lilies of the field, how they grow; they toil not, neither do they spin." Verse 29 says. " And yet I say unto you, That even Solomon in all his glory was not arrayed like one of these." God handles them. Matthew 6:30 (KJV) says, "Wherefore, if God so clothe the grass of the field, which to day is, and to morrow is cast into the oven, shall he not much more clothe you, O ye of little faith?"

Today, let your faith in God rise up and turn it over to Jesus.

88.

1. If your house note is past due.
2. If your car note is past due.
3. If your sister is holding a grudge against you.
4. If your people on your job are picking on you.
5. If you are sick in your body.
6. If your children won't act right.
7. If you have trouble with your car....won't start.
8. If your taxes are behind.

Whatever you do, have faith in God, keep working and turn it over to JESUS!

CHAPTER XVIX
GO THROUGH TO GET TO

You have to go through, to get to, the blessing. God never said it would be easy. (Mat 11:30 KJV) tells us, that Jesus said, "...my yoke is easy, and my burden is light. The way your burdens get light is to get in Jesus and leave them in the hands of the Lord.

Please allow me to give you two examples of 'go through to get to'. There was a man who loved this woman and they were engaged. One day he was over to her house visiting and it came time for him to go home. She asked him, "Harry, will you be back tomorrow to see me?" His reply was, "If it don't rain!" When it came time for their wedding day, she postponed it because she knew if he wouldn't come through a little rain for her, then he didn't really love her that much and he wouldn't be much of a husband anyway..

The late Dr. E. V. Hill, the man that I refer to as my pops, would always say, "If God can get it through ya, He will send it to ya; but if God can't get it through ya, then He won't send it to ya."

I found that to be so true. God won't bountifully bless people whose fist are closed because it indicates that they don't believe in 'seed time and harvest." They are selfish people. Their fist is always closed. When you sew seed, your hand must open up. When

89.

one 'goes through to get to', you cannot only receive, you must give too.

That is so much like the principal of 'go through to get to'. How can we as American people get to a higher level if we are not willing to 'go through to get to'? It works both ways. I know it's painful right now with this COVID 19; but no cross, no crown.
1 Thessalonians 5:18 says, "In every thing give thanks: for this is the will of God in Christ Jesus concerning you."

I have even been thanking God for this Coronavirus. Why????? Because the Good Book says that God made it. According to John 1:3 (KJV) "All things were made by him (the Lord); and without him was not any thing made that was made. I'm glad that the Lord made everything.....even the Coronavirus, because if God had allowed the enemy (the devil) to make the Coronavirus, that evil booger would have killed everyone on the face ot this earth. It could be worse than we think.

However, be of good courage. I believe that we are going 'through to get to'. We have to go through something to get to something. I believe that the people of America are:

1. Winners
2. Successful
3. Good giants
4. Good people
5. Overcomeers
6. Brothers and Sisters
7. More than conquerors
8. People who endure
9. Stead fast people
10. The head and not the tail
11. People who are going up, up, up!!!
12. People who desire to do right
13. People who have hope
14. People who love their brothers and sisters, no matter what color they are
15. People who give others a helping hand
16. Not jealous people and not envious people
17. Not liars
18. Not people who steal from each other
19. Real men and real women
20. People who GOD can get it through, He will send it to...... God is getting supplies to us, and we are sending it all over the nation and even helping other

21. nations....all over the world. God can get it through you because you are:

1. More than a conqueror.
2. You can do all things through Christ which strengthens you.
3. You are victorious.
   87.

4. It's not over for you.
5. You will make it.
6. It's going to be alright.
7. You are coming out of this Coronavirus with your hands up.
8. Cause you are a winner.
9. You are successful.
10. You will prosper.
11. You are blessed.
12. You are triumphant.
13. You are an over-comer.
14. You will conquer that thing.
15. The victory is in your hands.
16. You will stand.
17. You will continue.
18. You can't quit.
19. The battle is not yours.
20. It's the Lord's.
21. You are the head, not the tail
22. God is enlarging your territory.
23. God is taking you to new heights.
24. God is taking you to new depths.
25. God is taking you to new dimensions.
26. God is taking you to new realms.
29. God is taking you to new places.
30. God is giving you new opportunities.
31. God is taking you to new horizons.
32. God is giving you to new future.
33. You will be setting new goals.
34. God is opening new doors for you.
35. God is making new ways for you.
36. God is going to give you a better job.
37. God is giving you new promotions.

91.

38. God is giving you new blessings.
39. You've got a bright future.
40. And you've got your health back.
41. You've got your joy back.
42. You're <u>rejoicing</u> as never before.
43. You're <u>able to give</u> like you desire to give.
44. You're <u>able to travel</u> like you want to travel.
45. Instead of being broke, you've <u>got money.</u>
46. You are a person who weathers the storm.
47. You are a person who come through had trials.
48. You are a resilient person.
49. You are steadfast.
50. You are unmovable

I rebuke trouble in your home—I pray that you have:

1. No stickiness—the enemy cannot stick there—he cannot live there. He cannot--stay there—In the name of JESUS, get out!!!
2. I command trouble—to leave!
3. Arguments—go somewhere else!
4. Confusion—get out!
5. In fact, Police trouble—go somewhere else!
6. And even all thieves—go somewhere else!
7. I ask God to loose finances into your life!
8. Lord, not only cut the red tape, but deliver those finances in our hands....!
9. Release monies being held up!
10. Release some unexpected checks to the people !
11. Release inheritances!
12. Release money owed!
13. Release Pension checks held up!
14. Release financial chunks of money to the people!
15. Release disability checks!
16. Release government checks!
17. Release IRS checks!
18. Release support for the church!
19. Release the tithes and offerings!
20. Release IRS debt!
21. We are people who come up with vaccines!
22. We are people who don't give up!

GOD'S CURE TO THE CORONAVIRUS   Chief Ambassador Dr. Vernard Johnson

23. We are people who believe in God!
24. We are people who God has helped and blessed to beat other enemies like!
    a. Cancer b. Yellow fever, the Bubonic Plaque of San Francisco's China Town; the 1918 Flu, and all kinds of plaques and virus. We will find the health cure for COVID 19. We are just going through to get to!

Let us have hope and believe this, "We are well and not sick. We shall live and not die. God said we have dominion over all the earth and every thing that creepeth on the earth, and this thing (COVID 19) is creeping upon the earth. That means if we pray and believe God's word, something will happen to this COVID 19. God will zap it. I believe that.....join me. Meanwhile, we are going through to get to.

CHAPTER XX
I AGREE

The Word says, Amos 3:3 (KJV) declares "Can two walk together, except they be agreed?" Matthew 18:19 (KJV) says, "Again I say unto you, That if two of you shall agree on earth as touching any thing that they shall ask, it shall be done for them of my Father which is in heaven." I believe that God is going to help us defeat this Coronavirus. Can I get ANYBODY in America to agree with me???????????

In this chapter, I want to share with you a simple Rhema word that is extremely important....and if you will grab this thought and use it correctly, ultra awesome miracles will happen to you and all America. Are you ready for the word. The word is 'agree'.
Matthew 18:19 (KJV) says, "....That if two of you shall agree on earth as touching any thing that they shall ask, it shall be done for them of my Father which is in heaven.

The Word tells us in (1 John 5:8 KJV) And there are three that bear witness in earth, **the Spirit**, and **the water**, and **the blood**: and these three agree as one. Have you ever wondered why God said the Spirit, the water and the blood must agree, and what happens when they agree?

1. **When things agree, more of the power of God is present**. Leviticus 26:8 KJV) And five of you shall chase an hundred, and an hundred of you shall .

put ten thousand to flight: and your enemies shall fall before you by the sword. In Deuteronomy 32:30 KJV) Moses spoke these words to the Children of Israel when referring to them fighting their enemies. He asked them, "How should one chase a thousand, and two put ten thousand to flight, except their Rock had sold them, and the LORD had shut them up?" In other words, only GOD can do that. GOD is the one who helps His people work together and agree.....and there is more power among them who agree. One can chase a thousand...when you agree, and two can chase ten thousand when you........agree.

And when the spirit, the water and the blood agree, some mighty things happen. That's how huge mansions get washed off of the hills in Hollywood. God in the Spirit realm allows it....The water agrees with GOD. God permits the rain to fall and the water which agrees with God goes under those mansions and washes away the foundation, and the blood (which is the life), agrees with the

Spirit and the will of God, and with all three working together (the Spirit, the water and the blood working together) whatever God's grace and mercy permits as far as life is concerned, happens in that house that is washed off of that Hollywood hill. The house might be destroyed, but God saves the lives.

Listen, have you ever thought about when Jesus was hanging on the cross and the soldier pierced Him in the side, for this to have happened to Jesus, the Spirit had to get it from God in heaven....so it had to happen in the Spirit realm first, then the the water and the blood agreed with the Spirit.......and look at what happened....God allowed the soldier to pierce Jesus in His side (that was in the Spirit).....and what happened? Out came blood and water symbolized the washing away of sins through the precious blood of Jesus. You see that blood and water was for the saving and healing of the nations........and now, you are healed by the wound in His side. Hallelujah!!!! Your mama was healed, your daddy was healed, some of your loved ones were healed and now you are healed by the wound in His side......but the Spirit, the water and the blood had to agree.

Listen, lets try to agree at your church. Let's agree with the Leader, let's agree with the vision, and let's move to another level. Some churches could have been even father along, if some people were not stubborn and rebellious people who wanted to do only what they thought was right...not the vision of the leader. God gave the leader the vision, and you are not to be stubborn and rebellious but instead, follow your leader.

Not only, when things agree, there is more power of God present, but secondly,

2. **When people agree, it causes them to touch things together.** Just simply look at what happens when people touch things together, or touch people together. People are saved, healed, set free and delivered:
    a. That's why, while the Altar Call is going forth, the preacher ask you to 'pray saints', and even when the saints come up to pray, one lays hands on the person needing prayer, and the other saint lays hands on the back or shoulder of the person praying. You see, when they touch things together their prayers are answered....simply because the Word says, ".....as touching any thing that they shall ask....that's the second thing. Touch things together, and if you believe, something will happen.

3. **When people agree and ask of God miracles happen.** Mat. (Mat 7:7 KJV) "Ask, and it shall be given you; seek, and ye shall find; knock, and it shall be opened unto you: verse 8 says, "For every one that asketh receiveth; and he that seeketh findeth; and to him that knocketh it shall be opened. & (Mat 17:20b for verily I say unto you, If ye have faith as a grain of mustard seed, ye shall say unto this mountain, Remove hence to yonder place; and it shall remove; and nothing shall be impossible unto you.

4. **Believe that it shall be done for them of the Father which is in heaven.** You see, agreeing on earth, and touching things that you ask GOD for, moves God. It causes God to honor His Word and because it says right here in this chapter, "it shall be done for them (who is them....that's 'you'); and it shall be done for 'you' of my Father which is in heaven. The Father which is in heaven is moved by your agreeing on earth, and by your touching the same thing together in faith. He must honor his Word.
    a. **Example**.....that's why on this prayer line when we have SOS situations, sometimes we ask more than one person to pray. Example...one of the sons of an Ambassador was facing a long time in prison, but some of the people joined hands in the spirit realm and prayed for him.. After prayer, the judge reduced to a much less sentence. Why did that happen? I believe because "Jesus said, that if two of you shall agree, agree, agree on earth as touching, any thing that (we) shall ask, it shall be done for (us) of (the) Father which is in heaven." When the saints agree, on earth, that's when we can stand on Isaiah 55:11 (KJV) "So shall my word be that goeth forth out of my mouth: it shall not return unto me void, but it shall accomplish that which I please, and it shall prosper in the thing whereto I sent it." In the name of Jesus, "It shall be done unto you.....it shall happen!!!! Because we "agreed"!!!

95. I believe that America shall be victorious over this pandemic. Do you agree???

CHAPTER XXI
I'M DECLARING GROUND '0'

Very seldom in life does man always live on the mountain top. We all have our ups and downs. Sometimes there are things that come into all of our lives that completely knock us down. When that happens, we have to start at ground '0'. Life is full of valleys, pit falls, mountains and cliffs. Nevertheless, this is not so bad, because when we have to start at ground '0', the only place we can go from there is up.

I shall never forget when God spoke to my mind and told me and my family to leave Fort Worth, Texas. This was the most difficult decision I have ever made. We were doing so well in Fort Worth. We had a beautiful home with a marble front yard and a swimming pool with a saxophone in the bottom of it, we were driving beautiful cars, we had great influence, we made plenty of money, we had plenty of admirers and great friends, they knew me everywhere. I could walk in any church and they would stop their service for me.....we were truly blessed. But God said go to Kansas.

I did not understand why, in fact at first I thought it was the devil speaking to my heart, but when my wife started feeling the same way, I knew it was God speaking. So we left Fort Worth, Texas and started at ground '0' again. No, we don't have a beautiful house here in Kansas, and we are not driving a Mercedes Benz like in Texas, but let me tell you what has happened that I know would not have happened had we not obeyed God and started at ground '0' again:

1. We started a church called Amazing Grace. It is not a huge church but amazing things have happened there. In fact our motto is "Amazing things happen at Amazing Grace, and Amazing Grace is the place whee amazing things happen.
2. We started a Prayer Ministry with 4 people, but it has grown to over 200 countries that have linked on to it... and with the social media linking with us (Face Book, Twitter, Instagram, YouTube, LinkedIn, the UK, The Blog, K104 and numerous other radio stations, The Blog network reports that we now have a listening audience of over 1.7

billion listeners.
3. We have awesome influence among many churches.
4. Although we don't have a lot of money, God has truly made a way for us.
5. Out debt in Fort Worth was around 250,000, but with little income, our debt is now around 16,000. That is indeed a miracle.
6. We are changing the lives of millions of people.
7. Each night with the social media attached, we are sending up approximately 3 billion praises unto God.
8. I fasted 1,000 consecutive days.
9. I have written 7 books
10. We have made Ambassadors all over the country.
11. We are the ones who started people to thanking God 'a thousand times' a day.....and one of our Ambassadors (Bishop Patricia Stern) has thanked God over 10,000 times in 'one day'.
12. Kansas City is the place where God spoke to my heart and gave me the cure to the Coronavirus and inspired me to write this book.

All of this has come to pass since my wife and I followed the leading of the LORD, but we had to start from Ground '0'.

It looks like America is headed toward ground '0' right now, but be of good cheer, we might be headed toward ground '0' right now, but in due time, we will reach ground '100' , because 99 ½ just won't do.

CHAPTER XXII

A STEP DOWN TO STEP UP
(Judges 7:5-7)

INTRO:

In this chapter, I want to talk about "A Step Down To Step Up". Decree:

    a. **In your life,** I know you've been **wounded** and you've been **bruised**
    b. And sometimes you've **even had to weep**
    c. It **may have seemed like you were going down**
    d. But **don't worry about it. Be encouraged!**, because I've discovered that:
    'sometimes in life, the LORD will let you step down, in order, to step up.'

You can't be on the mountain top all the time. Life is not like that. Jesus never experienced that and God has never experienced that either. Do you think when the children of Israel committed Spiritual Adultery on God and were worshipping that golden calf, God had a good moment? Do you think when His son died on the cross, that was one of his good moments? God has some troublesome times too. Life is full of ups and downs. Even if you were to stay on the mountain top all the time, your mountaintop experiences would become a valley for you, because you must have the bad times to really appreciate the good times.

Some time ago I was on TBN (Trinity Broadcasting Station) as the special invited guest of the host that day.......and one of the things I said to her was, "Sometime ago I preached a sermon titled "A Step Down To Step Up", and while preparing for it, God showed me that every person has a different walk. Some walk:

    r. From side to side
    s. Happy walk
    t. Sad walk
    u. Tired walk
    v. Like they are angry at the world
    w. Never walk bent over, because people will ride your back.

And after watching several people walk, The Lord instructed me to watch:

    1. **The tops of their heads**—he showed me that in order to walk, **every person mus**

98.
> 2. **have a down and up motion**, ever so slight, side to side; but it's a down and up motion.
> 3. **Jump**—you have to go down, and the further down you go, **the higher you jump**.
>
> 4. [**SPIRITUAL APPLICATION**—every person here will have:]
>
>   a. Some ups and downs in life,
>   b. Some trouble and some storms,
>   c. Trouble will sometimes make you feel as though you are so far down that you can't come up.
>   d. And sometimes in life, the Lord will allow you to have:
>   Some trouble,
>   e. Some dark clouds before day light,
>   f. Your back against the wall,
>   g. To weep sometimes,
>   h. To be wounded and bruised,
>   But hang on in there. It's not over. It's only temporary. The Lord is just allowing you to step down, in order---- to step up.

Sometimes one has to experience some trouble before you will seek to be in His divine will rather than His permissive will. Sometimes one has to experience some dark clouds before the Lord can put you on the coarse to your divine destiny. Most of the time it is down in the valley, not on the mountaintop, when God can best get your attention. Oh, He can speak to you on the mountaintop too, but down in the valley there are fewer distractions. Up on the mountaintop people are constantly pulling on you:
Everybody wants something from you.
You are constantly bombarded with people who have problems
When the phone rings its people who want or need something

But when you are on the bottom you have fewer distractions and you are desperate to hear from God. It's like when a huge cold spell comes to Kansas. It gets rid of all the germs and bacteria that cause sickness because germs and diseases can't handle the cold. Well, when you are on the bottom, God uses it to get rid of things that are attacking your spiritual life and could cause you to be spiritually sick, and could keep you from reaching your divine destiny.

And then, most of the time it's down in the valley, not on the mountaintop when the Lord shapes you. That's when he prepares you for your mountaintop experiences
1. Sometimes when you are driving that hoopti that God is preparing you to drive something better
2. When you are not living on Sugar Hill that the Lord is getting you ready

99.
   3. Not wearing Lilly Ann dresses or Botany 500 suits that the Lord is shaping you
   4. Sometimes it is when it seems like you have stepped down the most that God is molding you, shaping you and making you into what He wants you to be.

That's why one has to be careful not to judge people who don't appear to be on top at the moment, because today they may be down, but tomorrow they may be up
Today-- usher in the lobby---tomorrow the gatekeeper for the King.
Today---driving a Pinto---tomorrow driving a Rolls Royce.
Placed in the bottom of the ditch by his brothers---tomorrow the person who has the bread in a famine
Today your tithes may be $10---tomorrow $10,000,000.

So when you are going through and people don't quite understand, just tell them,
"Please be patient with me, for God is not through with me yet
But when God get through with me (when God gets through molding and
shaping me), I shall come forth as pure gold.

   [You see, sometimes one has to experience some struggles before you will seek God:}

   1. Try to do **God's <u>divine</u> will** rather than His **<u>permissive will</u>**.
   2. Before the Lord can put you on **<u>the coarse to a purpose driven life</u>**.
   3. Most of the time it is **down in the valley**, not on the mountaintop, when God **can best get your attention.**

   Matter of fact, sometimes you ought to thank God when you are down and feel like a failure because all God uses are failures:

   1. Moses—killed an Egyptian—led the Children of Israel to the Promise Land
   2. David---Bathsheba---repented and became a man after God's own heart.
   2. Peter cursed in the Garden---repented and won 3,000 to Christ on the Day of Pentecost.
   3. **Let me put this on your street: <u>Steve McNair</u>**

      A few years ago, Steve McNair was the Quarterback that ended up in the Super Bowl; but his story is incredible. Five years before he got there, he worked in a grocery store stocking groceries; played Arena Football for 2 years overseas and in America; he came to the NFL as a back-up quarterback to Trent Green for the St. Louis Rams; but as fate had it, Trent Green was injured; Steve became the quarterback for the St. Louis Rams; led his team into winning their division and then led them into winning the Super Bowl. He was the division's MVP—Most Valuable Player and also won the MVP of the Super Bowl.

He was down, down, down, but he kept believing that God was going to bring him UP, UP, UP!!!

[Now, in order to substantiate this even further, let's got to the Word of God. There is a tremendous example of a group of people who can give a testimony that sometimes in life, the Lord will let you step down, in order to step up. It is found in Judges, chapter 6 & 7 so just for a few minutes, let us carefully peruse this.

The Principle Person: **God Jehovah**
Minor Persons: **Gideon and his men**
Geographical Setting: **Was by the well of Herod and by the hill of Moreh near a city called Ophrah Manesseh**
<u>Historicity</u> reflects:

1. The children of Israel did evil in the sight of the Lord and the Lord allowed the Midianites to place them in bondage for seven years.
2. Then Israel cried (prayed) unto God and the Lord sent them a deliverer—a prophet named Gideon, but Gideon **<u>needed a sure sign</u>** from the Lord that He would use him to deliver the children of Israel. So he put a fleece before the Lord. Gideon said, "Lord, I will place a wool fleece on the threshing floor, and let the fleece be wet and the ground all around it be dry; and God let it be so. Then Gideon changed the sign; he said to the Lord, if you will save Israel by my hand, then let the fleece be dry and the ground be wet and the fleece. The next morning, it was just as he had asked.
3. The Lord said unto Gideon the people are too many to go against the Midianites. Tell them that those who are afraid, go back to their home place; and **<u>twenty two thousand went back home</u>**.
4. Gideon went down to the camp of the Midianites with his servant Huhrah and they heard a man in the Midianite camp tell of a dream.
5. Trumpet in every man's hand with a **<u>trumpet in one hand and empty lamps in the other hand</u>**. **<u>Gideon divided the men into three groups and attacked the Midianites</u>** from three areas and gained the victory.

[While refreshing myself on this story, I was asking God, "Lord, what good can come from this story that can help our people better know that sometimes in life we have to step down in order to step up? And God seemed to show me three things. First of all, let them know that:]

1. God positions 'you' for victory

Look at verse 1 of the 7th chapter, it says, they, "pitched (or set up their camp) beside the well of Harod: so that the host of the Midianites were on the north side of them, by the hill of Moreh, in the valley—in the valley. There is some significance about the 'position' here. Look at where the enemy is positioned, down "... in the valley," but look at where the people of God are positioned, **up by the hill of Moreh**. Anyone knows that the vulnerable position is down in the valley. People can ambush you, attack you suddenly 'down' in the valley.

And can't you see**, that reveals Satan's strategy—to keep you down, down on yourself,** down **in your money,** down **in your bills,** down **with stress**, down with **pressures**, down with **burdens**, down **with depression** and down **with your self esteem**, down!

Listen**, the enemy plays mind games on you and tries to make you think that he is best positioned to help you, but in actuality, he's down in the valley**. Oh don't you hear Paul saying in Rom 16:20, "**And the God of peace shall bruise Satan under your feet shortly**. Listen, God positioned you for victory. The devil is down, down, down, but you are up, up, up!!! The enemy wants you to think he sits high and looks low, but it's God who sits high and looks low. The devil is down in the valley, but **God positioned 'you' for victory from on high**.

2. He that humbles himself shall be exalted.

(Judg 73--6 KJV) And the LORD told Gideon to send the soldiers with fear home, and yet there were too many. Ten thousand were left. Then God said, bring them down to the water, and I will try them for you. (Judg 7:5 NIV) So Gideon took the men down to the water. There the LORD told him, "Separate those **who lap the water with their tongues like a dog** from those who kneel down to drink." **Three hundred men lapped with their hands to their mouths**. All the rest got down on their knees to drink." **This was a test of humility.**

Example: "The Threshing Floor"—everyone was blessed; those that were standing and those who were down on their knees, but it was observed that **the women who were down on the Threshing Floor laying prostrate before the Lord were really blessed, simply because it showed a heart of total humility**. He that humbles himself shall be exalted.

3. **When you get a word from the LORD, move forward to your blessing.**

(Judg 6:39 NIV) Then Gideon said to God, "Do not be angry with me. Let me make just one more request. Allow me one more test with the fleece. This time make the fleece dry and the ground covered with dew." That night God did so. Only the fleece was dry; all the ground was covered with dew. Now look at what Gideon and his men did after this in Judges 7:1. "Then Jerubbaal, who is Gideon, and all the people that were with him, <u>rose up early</u>." **<u>This means that they were preparing to move to their blessing.</u>**

<u>Gideon received a definite sign from the Lord, **and when they did, they moved**. Listen, when GOD speaks to your heart, don't sit idle, move</u>!!!

Come here 'four lepers' who are sitting at the gates of the Syrians who said those famous words, **"Why sit we here until we die."** They sat there awhile and didn't see anybody, for GOD had <u>made the Syrians think that they heard</u> a **host of horses** and **chariots and a huge army coming after them** and they fled for their lives. The four lepers who at the gate said, "Why sit we here until we did?" We're hungry, and if we enter the city if there is no food, we will die there, and if we sit here at the gate, we will die here. Come on let us enter into the city. **They entered into the city and found all the food they could ever want. Listen, I believe that was a word from the Lord, and they moved on their blessing.**

Somebody is at a crossroads of life, and the devil is trying to tell you that it's not going to work and trying to minimize your faith; but just wait on the Lord, and when you know that you have a word from the Lord, **<u>move on your blessing</u>**!!!

My testimony: playing before President Clinton. Several years ago I was invited by the late Bishop L. H. Ford (Presiding Bishop of The Church Of God In Christ) to play my saxophone before President Clinton. The President was coming to speak at the Convocation.

Before I played, I said, "Mr. President, I have come to play your favorite song, "Amazing Grace". I know about God's amazing grace because I was born with asthma all down in my lungs, but my mother prayed for me and God healed me of asthma."

I put my song in my mouth and began to play "Amazing Grace". When I finished, the crowd and the President was giving me a standing ovation. I was standing on the upper stage, and that's when I heard a voice speaking to my mind, and it said, "Step down". I immediately stepped down off the upper stage to the level the President was on. I wasn't thinking about protocol, but the Holy Spirit knows about protocol when we don't know who to call.

When I stepped down off the higher stage, President Clinton stepped forward and shook my hand. Afterwards, I turned and walked to my seat on the platform. Then President Clinton motioned for me to come back to him. I went back over and The President gave me a hug and said some real encouraging things to me. I noticed that tears were flowing down his face when he hugged me. It was quite a moving experience.

When it was over, some things dawned on me. If I had not obeyed the Holy Ghost and stepped down when He spoke to me, I doubt if The President would have shook my hand. If I had not stepped down, I doubt if The President would have called me back and hugged me. If I had not stepped down, I doubt if The President would have said all the encouraging things to me, but I had to step down, in order.....................to step up!

Forgive me for being so demonstrative, but take your hand and **push yourself on the shoulder and shout, "Move to your blessing!!!** If there is anybody who has ever been down, but you got a word from the Lord, and you moved to a higher level, I know you completely understand what I am talking about.

[So when you are going through and people don't quite understand, just tell them, "Please be patient with me, for God is not through with me yet; but when God get through with me (when God gets through molding and shaping me), I shall come forth as pure gold."]

CHAPTER XXIII
GOD IS FIXING THINGS JUST FOR YOU

I know this is a simple topic for this chapter, but many times God uses simple things to confound the wise. "God Is Fixing It Just For You." During this time of a pandemic, I don't know of any stronger topic I can speak on to encourage you. God really is "Fixing Things Just For You". Be encouraged!!!!!

God is fixing things just for you—He's repairing things, he's making things right, He's resolving things, He's settling some things, He's handling the situations, He's fixing things just 'for you'. I don't know about you, but 'I' need some things fixed, and the Lord wants me to tell you:

If you've been trying to purchase something and you are worried about your credit. . .
If you've got a money problem and you can't seem to make ends meet, if you will work and remember God's bride....the church:

The Bible says God will fix it for you.
If somebody did you wrong and it hurt you to your heart, just know that God is fixing it just for you.
If you've been sick and the doctor can't seem to fix your problem, know that God is fixing it just for you.
If you are hurting deep down inside and you can't seem to get rid of the pain, know that God is fixing it just for you.
If you've got some problems on their job, know that God is fixing it just for you.
I know you have a problem that's been worrying you for some time, but know that God is fixing it just for you.
If you've got some troble somewhere and you've been almost pulling your hair out because you don't know what to do, know that God is fixing it just for you.
If you have an unspoken request that you don't want to tell anybody, know that God is fixing it just for you.

God wants me to tell you that "He's fixing it just for you; and if there is anyone who will receive this chapter, just say that to yourself or out loud, "He's fixing it for me."

[There is a scriptural example that I I surmised 3 principles from. These principles ill help you to better know that He's fixing it for you. So just for a few minutes during this chapter, let us carefully peruse this chapter, perspicaciously examine it, apply it to your life, and also extract some meat from it that shall be spiritual food for our souls.

The Principal Character:	Nehemiah
The Minor Characters:	King Artaxerxis
Geographical Setting:	Jerusalem in the province of Judah; 30 miles SE of Joppa and 25 to 30 miles NE of Lachish
Time Line	This happened around 440 BC (before birth of Jesus, the Christ).
Historicity:	Reflects that:

Hanani, one of the Jewish brethren was returning from Jerusalem with some of his men and Nehemiah asked him about Jerusalem and about the remnant of Jews that had survived the Babylonian exile under king Nebuchadnezzar. He received some discouraging news. Hanani told him that things were horrible. He said those who survived the exile and are back in the province and are in great trouble and disgraced. Then he said the wall of Jerusalem is broken down, and its gates have been burned with fire." When Nehemiah heard this, he was devastated. This was the city that Nehemiah loved and when Nehemiah heard this, he sat down and wept. Then for several days, he mourned and fasted and prayed before the God of heaven. However, God gave him the vision to go to Jerusalem and repair the wall of the city. He began the work, and when the men of Jerusalem came together, each tribe and family joined in and helped to repair a portion of the wall, God gave them the victory.

[Now, there are some profound things that we can learn from Nehemiah's experience:

1. Let God see your tears:

Look at verse 4 of chapter 1, "When I heard these things, I sat down and wept." Now here is a man weeping—a man of God so concerned for the people of God that he weeps. You can say what you want to say, but **sincere tears move God**:

Jeremiah said in Jer 9:1, "Oh that my head were waters, and mine eyes a fountain of tears, that I might weep day and night for the slain of the daughter of my people!" Remember in Judges 20:6 how the Gibeonites raped and killed the concubine of that Levite man, and the Levite man was so distraught that he cut her up and sent her body parts to each region of Isreal. The

106.

Gibeonites and Isreael went to war over that and at first the Gibeonites were winning, but in Judges 20:23, the Bible says Israel went before the Lord and began to weep, and then they fasted and prayed and God gave them the victory. In Luke 7:38, when the woman who had lived a sinful life washed the feet of Jesus with her tears and then dried them with her hair? The Pharisees criticized Jesus because he let this sinner woman touch him, but Jesus rebuked them and then He forgave this woman's sins, simply because of the sincerity of her tears.

When Jesus died, Mary stood at the tomb of Jesus weeping and the two angles appeared and asked her why she was crying. She said, "They have taken my Lord away, and I don't know where they have put him." The next thing she knew, when she turned around, Jesus, Himself appeared unto her and consoled her. Why? I believe Jesus saw her tears.
After the rooster crowed on Peter, the Bible said, "He wept bitterly," because he had denied the Christ, but Jesus saw his tears, and the next thing we know is that on the Day of Pentecost, Peter preached to the multitude and won over 3,000 souls to Chirst. God saw his tears
When Mary and Martha, the sisters of Lazarus came to Jesus, they were weeping and Mary said, "Lord, if you had been here, my brother would not have died. . . . .continue.
In John 11:35, after Jesus watched Mary and her friends weeping over the death of Lazarus, Jesus was moved with compassion and the Bible says, "Jesus wept." Psalms 30:5 says, "Weeping may endure for a night, but joy comes in the morning."

Oh, I remember so well two Christmas's ago, when it looked as though our family was going to have a bleak Christmas. I had stopped traveling to stabilize the Church, my wife had quit her job as Manager of Job Employment for Missouri and it just looked like our family wasn't going to have much of anything for Christmas. Then the Sunday before Christmas, the Church surprised us with $500.00. I was alright until my wife started crying. Before I knew it, big tears started swelling up in my eyes and it took everything in me to hold the tears back. Her tears moved me. All I'm trying to tell you is that every now and then you need to let God see your tears. If they are sincere, they will move God to make a way out of no way.

2. Learn how to mourn--mourning will get God's attention:

Matthew 5:4 (KJV) "Blessed are they that mourn: for they shall be comforted."
Look at the B portion of verse 4, "and mourned certain days." When Nehemiah heard the lamentation of his brothern he began to mourn and he did it for several days.
Matthew 5:4 says, "Blessed are they that mourn, for they shall be comforted." Even the Lord said in Jeremiah 9:17 (KJV), ". . .call for the mourning women, that they may come; and let them make haste, and take up a wailing for us, that our eyes may run down with tears, and our

107.

eyelids gush out with waters." Listen, mourning will get God's attention. It shows that you are passionate about something. That you are troubled— That your heart is grieved and that you are desperate to hear from God. When you get desperate, God will show up. For some of you that think mourning is not appropriate, Eccl 3:4 says "There is, "A time to weep, and a time to laugh; a time to mourn."
Prov 29:2 says, "When the righteous are in authority, the people rejoice: but when the wicked beareth rule, the people mourn."

Why is it important that people mourn? People all over America and the world have lost loved ones and they are mourning. I believe this is going to get God's attention. Why is this significant? GOD can help us.

We <u>don't mourn anymore about sin</u>. The Church now has compromised so much and embraced the world so much, until we have forgotten about how to mourn about the travesties of sin. When Nehemiah saw how sin had broken his people, how just a remnant was left, how the walls of the city were broken down and the gate to the city was burned, he not only wept but he began to mourn. <u>Mourning is a step further than weeping</u>. Weeping is simply sheading tears from your eyes, but <u>mourning is showing grief, to lament, to bemoan, to bewail, to open your mouth and express great sadness about something.</u> .

In Nehemiah's day, they would tear their clothes, throw ashes on their heads, rather than wearing fine clothing they would dress down in sackcloth, just to show their grief over something. Where are the saints who are grieved about the way our nation is going. Today, in our nation we have:

One murder—every 20 seconds
One rape—every 10 seconds
One robbery—every 8 seconds
One mugging—every 2 seconds somewhere in our nation
The abortion rate is increasing
Our youth are walking around looking mean because of gangster rappers
Every since two famous women kissed on nation-wide television, our young ladies in high school across the country are becoming lesbians

It seems like our girls have gone wild—women liking women. The bible says they won't enter the kingdom of God.
Our young men are embracing homosexuality—men liking men; and now it's <u>spreading rapidly throughout the church</u>

108.

Men are even marring men and women marring women

Where are the saints that are going to mourn for our nation—for the Church??? I remember the old senior saints who you could hear saying, "Oh, oh, oh, oh God! And they would say it until they got God's attention. Where are those saints today; and where are the Amazing Grace saints who are going to mourn for Amazing Grace; mourn for the sinful ways of our people, mourn for lost souls, mourn until God sends men from the east and west; mourn until God saves to the uttermost? Mourn and weep until God opens the windows of heaven and blesses us, Mourn for Amazing Grace until God smiles on us and shows us more favor!!!!

3. Keep on fasting and praying:

That's what Nehemiah did. Look at that same verse, Neh 1:4, the C part of the verse, KJV) And it came to pass, when I heard these words, that I sat down and wept, and mourned certain 106.

days, and fasted, and prayed before the God of heaven." Look at this! Nehemiah is giving us the keys to getting God to fix things for us. He says he let God see his tears, then he began to mourn, and then he fasted and prayed.

Notice that the last thing Nehemiah says is that he fasted and prayed. Listen, you pull out your big weapons at the end. If the small artillery won't work, you have to pull out your cannons. I believe he's trying to tell us to 'yes', combine all these things together, but if weeping won't do it; if mourning won't do it; then I dare you to fast and pray. It will get the job done:

>   Little prayer—little power
>   Some prayer—some power
>   Much prayer—much power
>   Little fasting—little power
>   Some fasting—some power
>   much fasting—much power.......tell somebody, "I want much power."

Prayer is talking with God; and if you want God to fix it, I dare you to have a talk with Jesus, and tell Him all about your trouble. He will here your faintest cry and answer you by and by.

Testimony: Orchestra. . . . For years it was my privilege to be The Executive Director of the Instrumental Music Division of the Church Of God In Christ. We had a list of 2,500 musicians in our data base, but we could only perform with a 100 piece orchestra. when the Church moved to The Fed Ex Forum for the Convocation. . . The Orchestra was placed in the

109.

nose bleed section because they had grown too large and there was no room on stage for them.

When my adjutants told me this, I found me a room directly behind the stage and I told GOD all about it. Then I began to thank God in advance for fixing it for us. We had spent hours and days rehearsing and now we were being told that there was no space for us because we had grown too large. It hurt really bad.

However, as I was behind the stage praying, one of the Orchestra men came running to where I was and said, "DR. JOHNSON, IT'S A MIRACLE!!!! THEY HAVE MOVED THE ORCHESTRA RIGHT IN FRONT OF THE STAGE. That had never happened in the history of the Church Of God In Christ. To do this, they had to moved the Superintendents and some Bishops, making The Orchestra one of the main focal points of the entire Convocation. GOD used the late Bishop G. E. Patterson to do this, and I shall never forget it. Many of the officials were angry, but I know the LORD fixed it for us. As I remember how

GOD fixed it for us, tears are streaming down.....and I KNOW since GOD fixed it for us, He will fix it for 'you'. I shall never forget when they gave the Orchestra the opportunity to play a song, we were ready! God led me to have the Orchestra to play "Oh The Glory", and the GLORY of the Lord truly came down. I can't help but shed tears as I look back on that day.....and just like GOD fixed it for us, He can fix it for you. It may be rough right now, and you may be at a turning point and don't know what to do, but I am a living witness that GOD can fix it just for you!

When you fast and pray, fasting and praying <u>will move God</u> to:

    Fix it just for you.
    Break the bonds of sin.
    Shake things lose.
    Cause God to open doors for you—new opportunities.
    Give you joy instead of sorrow.
    Cause God to enlarge your territory.
    Give you a greater anointing.
    Give you victory.
    Make the devil step back and leave you alone.
    Give you power.
    Make you blessed and not cursed.
    Cause God to turn things around.
    Cause God to fix things for you.

Prayer changes things. I'm going to pray until God moves.

The Word of the Lord says in Matthew 17:21"This kind goeth not out but by prayer and fasting". Luke 18:1 says, "Men ought always to pray, and not faint." James 5:16 proclaims "The effectual fervent prayer of a righteous man availeth much;" and James 5:14-15 says, "Is any sick among you? let him call for the elders of the church; and let them pray over him, anointing him with oil in the name of the Lord: Verse 15 continues, "And the prayer of faith shall save the sick, and the Lord shall raise him up; and if he have committed sins, they shall be forgiven him." JESUS can fix it just for you.

CHAPTER XXIV
A Breakthrough Is Coming

The Principal Person:: God Jehovah
The Minor Persons: Abraham & Sarah
The Geographical Setting: This happened in the land of Canaan

The Time Line Around the time that Moses wrote the Pentateuch, 1446

The Historicity: Reflects that

There was a couple that fell in love. They got married and they were very happy. Through the Spirit realm I sense that they were inseparable. Wherever Abraham went, you would find Sarah, and wherever Sarah went, you would find Abraham nearby. I don't know if they dressed alike or did anything like that, but I believe they loved each other and they had each others back.

In her day, Sarah must have been very beautiful...so beautiful that Abraham asked her to lie and say that she was his sister to keep him from being killed; but just like everyone else, Sarah had a problem. She couldn't have any children. And in the day in which they lived, if a woman couldn't have children, she was looked down on. Sarah was so desperate to have children, she sent her husband in to lay with her handmaid Hagar (an Egyptian woman). She conceived and had a son. They called her son Ishmael. Some time after that, Sarah conceived a healthy baby boy. They named him Issac.

[Now, how did the breakthrough come. There was a process. And today, I want to give you three simple things that Abraham and Sarah did to get their breakthrough; and I want to assure you that if you will listen and do these three things, without a doubt, a breakthrough will come to your life.. Here are the three things:

When God tells you something, don't laugh

(Gen 17:15 KJV) And God said unto Abraham, As for Sarai thy wife (she was later called Sarah), thou shalt not call her name Sarai, but Sarah shall her name be. (Gen 17:16 KJV) And I will bless her, and give thee a son also of her: yea, I will bless her, and she shall be a mother of nations; kings of people shall be of her. (Gen 17:17 KJV) Then Abraham fell upon his face, and laughed, and said in his heart, Shall a child be born unto him that is an hundred years old? and shall Sarah, that is ninety years old, bear? In Gen 18:12, when Sarah heard the angel say this, Sarah laughed. So both the husband and the wife laughed.

Num 23:19 tells us that, "God is not a man, that he should lie; neither the son of man, that he should repent: hath he said, and shall he not do it? or hath he spoken, and shall he not make it good?"

(Gen 17:18 KJV) And Abraham said unto God, O that Ishmael (my other son by Hagar) might live before thee! Verse 19, "And God said, Sarah thy wife shall bear thee a son indeed; and thou shalt call his name Isaac: and I will establish my covenant with him for an everlasting covenant, and with his seed after him."

Don't try to do it your way—do it God's way.

I mentioned earlier that In Genesis 16, Abraham and Sarah could not have any children, so Sarah wanted children so badly, she suggested to her husband, that he should go in unto her hand maiden, Hagar. They were doing it their way. Abraham went in and Hagar became pregnant and had a son named Ishmael. (Gen 17:18 KJV) And Abraham said unto God, O that Ishmael (my other son by Hagar) might live before thee! Verse 19, "And God said, Sarah thy wife shall bear thee a son indeed; and thou shalt call his name Isaac: and I will establish my covenant with him for an everlasting covenant, and with his seed after him."

112.

Never give up and never stop trying!

(Gen 21:1 KJV) And the LORD visited Sarah as he had said, and the LORD did unto Sarah as he had spoken. Verse 2, "For Sarah conceived, and bare Abraham a son in his old age, at the set time of which God had spoken to him.
 (Gen 21:2 KJV) For Sarah conceived, and bare Abraham a son in his old age, at the set time of which God had spoken to him."

(Gen 21:3 KJV) And Abraham called the name of his son that was born unto him, whom Sarah bare to him, Isaac.

Abraham was 86 when he had his last child by Hagar (Sarah's handmaid). We know that because he was now 99 when God spoke to him about Sarah and his youngest son Ishmeal (born of Hagar, Sarah's mistress or handmaid) was now 13. But it is quit evident that Abraham never gave up and he never stopped trying, because at age 100, just as the angel of the Lord had promised, Sarah conceived a child. They called his name Isaac.
It was that great English stateman, (who was face with what looked like defeat of his country, England, who was fighting Hitler's Germany in World War II. France had fallen and it seemed as though the Nazis were unstoppable, but Churchill stood up at the mic and gave a "3" word speech that changed the course of the war. He said, "Never give up!"

When it looks impossible, that's when a breakthrough is coming

Abraham was 100 and Sarah was close to 90. It looked impossible, but that's when the breakthrough came. Sarah had a son.

It may look like it's never going to happen.............It looks like we are never going to get out of this pandemic.........

We are in an old, old building, and it looks like we will never get out.....but I feel a breakthrough coming.

I believe Matthew 18:19. "Whatever I lose on earth shall be loose in heaven, so as I close this book, I am taking time to lose on you blessings like you have never experience before. I lose blessings on your family too. May you be:

   Blessed in the city,
   Blessed in the field.
   May your going out be blessed.

May your family be blessed.
May you be blessed with great health.
May you be blessed with great strength.
May your home be blessed.
May your automobile be blessed.
May you be blessed when you travel.
May you be blessed when you return home.
May everything you touch be blessed.
And may you be blessed, blessed, blessed, blessed, BLESSED!!!!!!!

I'm tired of the devil walking. I tired of the devil pressing you down. I'm loosing a breakthough on you, and it's coming in your life. You've had enough heartaches. You've had enough pains. You've had enough . . . . . . You need a breakthough, and it's coming. All you have to do is just live right, and "Be not weary in well doing . . . . . , Gal 6:9"

CHAPTER XXV
CONTINUOUS PRAISE

(Luke 18:1 KJV) And he spake a parable unto them to this end, that men ought always to pray, and not to faint;

(Luke 18:2 KJV) Saying, There was in a city a judge, which feared not God, neither regarded man:

(Luke 18:3 KJV) And there was a widow in that city; and she came unto him, saying, Avenge me of mine adversary.

(Luke 18:4 KJV) And he would not for a while: but afterward he said within himself, Though I fear not God, nor regard man;

(Luke 18:5 KJV) Yet because this widow troubleth me, I will avenge her, lest by her continual coming she weary me. Matthew 6:8, ". . . for your Father knoweth what things ye have need of, before ye ask him. Matthew 7:7 says, "Ask, and it shall be given you; seek, and ye shall find; knock, and it shall be opened unto you:

114.

1 John 5:15 tells us, "And if we know that he hear us, whatsoever we ask, we know that we have the petitions that we desired of him."

Recently, the Lord asked me to <u>do something that I didn't understand</u>. I was thinking, 'If I can just do the things that I do understand, I think that should be alright, but it's the things that I don't understand that baffle me. Nevertheless, I obeyed God.

Let me ask you this question. <u>How does one rejoice when there is a Red Seas before you</u>, mountains on your left and right and Pharaoh and his army (your enemies) in hot pursuit behind you? <u>Perhaps this decree will help us. Please make this decree to yourself, or out loud if you can:</u>

>God wants me to rejoice in the Lord always
>Even when I don't understand certain things
>Because in every situation I face
>If I give it to God
>I will have the victory.

As I thought about that decree, I felt led to challenge all of us to check God's record:

>When has the Lord ever left you or forsaken you?
>When has the Lord ever lost a battle?
>When has the Lord ever failed you?
>When has the Lord not come through for you?
>When has the Lord not healed you?
>When has the Lord not helped you with your finances?
>When has the Lord not supplied your every need?
>When has the Lord not seen you through your storms?
>When has the Lord not blessed you?
>When has the Lord not fought your battles?
>When has the Lord not helped you on your job?
>When has the Lord not answered your prayer?
>When has the Lord not fed you when you were hungry?
>When has the Lord not made a way for you out of no way?
>When has the Lord not clothed you when you were naked?
>When has the Lord not seen you through your darkest nights?
>When has the Lord not let you overcome your enemies?

The things above give all of us several reasons to give God continuous praise. So "rejoice in

115.

the Lord 'always'. 'Always' is a kind of futuristic word. Down here on this earth, it means 'forever', up in heaven it means for eternity or until the end of time, but at the same time, <u>it means 'at all times', or just continuously.</u> So when our chapter says, "Rejoice in the LORD always," God means for us to <u>rejoice in the Lord forever, rejoice in the Lord for eternity, til the end of time, at all times and rejoice in the Lord continuously.</u> Even if some things are going wrong. Even if people are dying, Even if we are sick. Even if we have a pandemic with Coronavirus.

I recently did a sermon titled, "<u>A Thousand Times Thank You,</u>" and in that sermon I mentioned that I have thanked the Lord at least a thousand times a day for over a thousand days; but during those thousand days, I must admit that there were times I wondered, "Lord, why am I thanking you." Then I realized,<u> if you rejoice in the Lord continuously, you won't miss it.</u> Miss what? <u>There are so many things that God does for us that we are unaware of; and if we knew what they were, we wouldn't want to miss thanking God for them.</u> I listened to the testimony of my late mother (Mother Adlee Johnson) in her hospital bed. Mother Johnson said, "I was having problems with my legs. I was exercising every day. Even though they were hurting, in the morning before I got up I would exercise them. Then I would get up and exercise them, but I <u>didn't know that I had eight blood clots in my leg, and if just one of them moved on up to my heart or brain and burst,</u> I might not have been here today she said. But the Lord took good care of me." <u>Then she began to cry and say, "Oh, thank you Jesus...thank you Jesus...thank you JESUS!!!"</u>

She didn't know she had blood clots, but GOD knew it. When I heard her testimony I began to understand why the Lord said "Rejoice in the Lord always." Listen, regardless of the situation, if there is a thank you on your lips, you won't miss giving God thanks for what He does for you. Some person reading this book has had miracle after miracle, after miracle, but you considered them little small things, so you missed giving God the thanks that you owe Him. Let me give you some examples:

1. Perhaps you lost your purse, or wallet, or even your keys. You searched everywhere and could not find them, but you asked God to help you, and the Lord helped you to find them. It was such a little thing you didn't recognize it was a miracle, but since you know it now, you ought to give God some praise.
2. Perhaps you almost ran out of <u>gas. It was the Lord that reminded you that you were low, but you forgot to thank Him.</u>
3. <u>Somebody may have had</u> a <u>flat tire and help came. It was the Lord that sent you the help, but you didn't recognize it. So you didn't give Him thanks.</u>

116.

4. Perhaps your <u>car just stopped</u>, but God sent somebody to help you and didn't charge you a dime.
5. Perhaps you had a flat, or like me, a blow out doing 70 miles per hour. It was God who kept you from killing yourself. I gave Him some praise. Can you stop right now and give God some praise.
   You have had things to happen that you considered such <u>little things that</u> you didn't recognize they were miracles, but since you know it now, you ought to celebrate the Lord.
6. Perhaps, the police stopped you for a ticket, and he gave you a warning, You were frustrated, but you didn't realize that God just kept you from having a fatal accident.
7. You had trouble on your job and God made the enemy behave.
8. Perhaps your X spouse wouldn't pay child support, but God supplied your every need just when you needed it.
9. You got fired on your job and you were so frustrated you almost cursed, but now many people on that job have the Coronavirus. You better thank God.
10. You got the Coronavirus but you didn't have the right insurance to go to the hospital, so you had to stay at home and quarantine yourself. God may have saved your life. In everything give thanks.
11. Some things seemed like such little things that you didn't recognize that God was doing a miracle for you. He may have saved your life. Again, why don't you stop and give God thanks.
12. The Senate and the Congress just passed a 2 trillion dollar bill to help all Americans. You thanked the Senate in your heart. You thanked the Congress in your heart; but 111
13. did you give thanks to GOD too! Why don't you <u>openly</u> give God thanks!

We miss recognizing the miracles that GOD does for us. In fact, perhaps somebody reading this book is <u>about to miss it right now, because maybe someone around you has the Coronavirus, but you are sitting there reading this book feeling fine. That's a miracle. You ought to take a praise break and give GOD some praise</u> right now!!! Don't give Him any <u>cute praise</u> because we are not going through a <u>cute situation</u>. We are going through a war, and when you are going through a war, you ought to give God a war cry. Thank you LORD!!!!!!!

The revelation that the Lord gave me to support the idea of 'continuous praise' concerning this topic, "Rejoice in the Lord always," is indeed an unusual one. The story is found in the Bible, Revelations 4:6-11; and for a few minutes let us carefully peruse this chapter, apply it to my life, then exact some meant from the chapter that shall be spiritual food for all of our souls.

The Principal Character: Is God, Jehovah

Minor Characters:	Are John (the revelator) The four beast that sit around the throne of God, and the twenty four elders.
The Time Line	This happened around 95 A.D. (after the death of Jesus)
Geographical Setting:	Between two settings: on the Isle of Patmos, and Heaven
The Historicity:	Reflects that:

John the Revelator lived during a time when Rome was in power around 95 A.D.; and the Romans sought to enforce Emperor worship. They contended that Caesar was Lord, whereas John the Revelator and other Christians preached that Jesus is Lord. For this, he was exiled to the Isle of Patmos, and on the Isle of Patmos God showed him a vision of Eschatology (things that deal with death, judgment, heaven & hell). His vision was apocalyptic (a warning about the coming disasters & judgments) and symbolic. He saw many things such as seven golden lamp stands (representing 7 churches), seven stars (representing 7 angels), the throne of God, and the twenty four thrones around His throne, and on them sat the twenty four elders. Then in John's vision, in Revelations 4:6, John saw four beast, or four living creatures with eyes in front and in back, around the throne.

The first living creature was like a lion, the second was like an ox, the third had a face like a man, the fourth was like a flying eagle. Each of the four beast had six wings and was covered with eyes all around, even under their wings. Day and night they never stop saying: "Holy, Holy, Holy is the Lord God Almighty, who was, and is, and is to come." And after the four beast give thanks to God, the twenty-four elders that sit before the thrown, fall down before him and worship him. They lay their crowns before the throne and worship the Lord. Again, this is the revelation that John saw on the Isle of Patmos.

[Now, what can we learn from four beast sitting around the throne of God, and the twenty four elders. What can four beast teach us about 'continuous praise'? I contend that there is much to be learned from them, but I want to suggest four things; and in order to see these four principles best, we must look at them in retrograde (backwards). First of all these beast can teach us that:

1. **God is relevant for today**,,, Hebrews 13:8 (KJV) proclaims, "Jesus Christ the same yesterday, and to day, and forever."

   God IS relevant for today. Look at verse 8 of Revelations Chapter 4 in retrograde. The last thing that the 4 beast say in that verse is "... who was, and is, and is to come." He's relevant! God 'was' which means that He was before the world was. In fact God was before 'was' was; and when He stepped out on nothing-less, hurled the sun into place . and called the light day and the darkness night, he did it because He 'was'. You have to understand that 'was' couldn't have been 'was' before God 'was', because God was the one who put the 'w' in 'was', the 'a' in was, and the 's' in was. So God was before was 'was'.

And not only was God 'was', but God 'is'. That means He's relevant for right now'! I remember hearing about an old country black preacher down in Mississippi who didn't know how to speak English too well, but he was preaching about the word 'is'. His message went something like this:

"This morning, my brothers and sisters, I want to preach about 'Is'. Now 'is' ain't no nown; and 'Is' ain't no pronoun. 'Is' ain't no adjective, and 'Is' ain't no conjunction. But 'Is' is just 'IS'!!!

Like, 'I is', and like 'You is', and like 'We is' children......is I'm right or is I'm wrong?

He preached about 'is' a little while longer, and then he started walking down the isle closing his message as he asked the people,

"Is you gonna sit at the welcome table??? I said children, Is you gonna sit at the welcome tabe??? I know I is, yeah I is, but the question is.........Is you????" Then he asked them, "Is I'm right, or is I'm wrong???

My point is.......even though that old black preacher didn't know the English language too well.............One thing he did know..........he knew that GOD is!!!

1. God is the one that made the world. All the doctors, scientist, the Admiral, and Generals

   didn't even know they were in the world until they came out of their mother's womb and woke up in the world. The world was already there. God put it there, so give GOD his props too.

2. God is the one who created man and woman. Genesis (the book of beginnings) tells us in Genesis 1:26-27 (KJV) gives us history as it proclaims, " And God said, Let us make man in our image, after our likeness: and let them have dominion over the fish of the sea, and over the fowl of the air, and over the cattle, and over all the earth, and over every creeping thing that creepeth upon the earth." This Coronavirus is creeping upon

119.

the earth, and Mr. President, we win this war because GOD gave us dominion over it!

Now, that's important to know, because there are some people who are trying to change the Bible and make everything God said in His word obsolete. Don't allow them to influence you, Mr. President. God and His Word can give you even more power than you ever thought existed. The Apostle Paul said in Hebrews 13:8, Jesus Christ the same yesterday, and to day, and for ever. Everything Jesus did yesterday is applicable and valid for today's world. Don't let anyone make you think just because the world is changing that the Lord changes too. There's a new terminology for almost everything:

Courting—dating,
Beat up or getting mugged—assaulted,
Lying and lies—just another viewpoint,
People playing mind games on other folks—'playas',
Molecular studies and cloning, is now being called 'stem cell research',
Punks, sissies and fagots are now called homosexuals and 'an alternate lifestyle',
Bull Diggers, dikes, are now called lesbians and 'an alternate lifestyle'.

But I want you to know that Jesus is the same, yesterday, today and forever more. His power has not diminished. The same GOD who opened the Red Sea and allowed the Children of Israel to walk through it, can tell the Coronavirus to leave the world and it WILL leave the world. The same GOD that put buoyancy in the water and allowed Peter to walk on the water,
116,

can order this pandemic to cease in the world and it WILL cease. Mr. President, put your trust in God....acknowledge Him, just as you acknowledge the doctors, scientist, Admirals, and Generals, and HE will come to your rescue. Second, these four beast can teach us to:

2. Remember that <u>God is almighty</u>

Also in verse 8 it says that He is "Lord God Almighty." I believe the reason why God wanted me to tell you this is because we have some people that appear as though they have forgotten this. If they haven't, why is it that when trouble rises, they start shaking in their boots. They act as though they don't have any faith; and the Bible says, "Without faith, it's impossible to please God."

The chapter says, "Lord God Almighty." Now, the writer of the chapter could have stopped at Lord. He could have stopped with God, but he didn't. He goes on to call Him, "Almighty." There is a reason for that.Could it be that the Word is trying to remind us that every battle you are fighting, count it a victory.Why ? Because <u>the Lord is almighty</u>—He's omnipotent—all-powerful—<u>there ain't nothing He can't</u> do.

Testimony: I shall never forget what our daughter (Lynitra) said when shee was 5 years old.

120.

At the time, we lived in Fort Worth, Texas. It was quite unusual, but it snowed a little, barely covering the ground. Lynitra had never seen snow and she was sooooooo excited!!! Then she said, "Daddy, Daddy, please make me a snow man." I replied, "Baby, it didn't snow enough for me to make you a snow man. I can't make you a snow man." Lynitra stood there looking out the window and with tears just rolling down her face said with a very tearful voice, "But I know MY Daddy can make a snow man, cause MY Daddy can do ANYTHING. Mr. President, I went and found me a board and scraped snow from all around the back yard, all around the pool and the sidewalks until I had enough snow to make a snow man. It didn't look like much and it had grass sticking out of it from the yard, but I made a snow man.

When Lynitra came outside, she was sooooooooooooooooooooooooooooooo happy and excited!!!!!!!!!!! She jumped up and down and shouted with a loud voice, "See there, I knew MY Daddy could make a snow man, I knew MY Daddy could make a snow man!!!!!
Mr. President, history records that your late Daddy was a great man and he could make a snow man; but he is gone. Now your Daddy is GOD and He can really make a snow man. He can even stop this Coronavirus. Just lead our nation and the world in prayer, and ask Him to. Not only can these four beast teach us that God is relevant for today, and that God is almighty, but thirdly these beast can teach us that:

3. **Continuous praise is a prerequisite for heaven:**

Look at Rev 4:8, ". . . and they (the four beast in heaven) rest not day and night, saying, Holy, holy, holy." They <u>rest not</u> day and night, not day, not day, not day, and night, and night! Listen, I want to make an announcement, **"If you don't like to praise God, and if you are ashamed of God, and if you don't like Christians, cancel your reservation for heaven, because continuous praise is a prerequisite for heaven."** **The people in heaven will be praising God all the time.** The Word tells us that He inhabits the praises of His people.

David said in Psalms 67:3 (KJV) "Let the people praise thee, O God; let all the people praise thee." The Bible teaches us that there aren't but two places you can go, heaven or hell. So, if you're not going to heaven, then that means that in hell you will lift up your eyes. God is going to have Him a people who will praise Him.

Just the other day, I experienced something that I have never experienced before. I asked the Lord, "<u>Lord, why is it that the devil tries to keep people in the church from praising you</u>???" And God showed me that <u>shouting praises</u> unto God <u>confuses the devil.</u> He can't understand how a person can shout praises unto God when your house note is due. He can't understand how a person can be sick in their body and shout praises unto God, or when he's been

121.

attacking you all week long and you are still happy and shouting. It confuses the enemy, that's why he's trying to keep you quiet right now—he doesn't want to be confused. The enemy is confused because:

1. He has given America It's best shot to make it fall, but America is still standing.
2. He has tried his best to discourage America but America is still singing, "God Bless America"
3. He has tried his best to put a curse on America, but the curse has been reversed.
4. I just left Wal Mart an hour ago. I needed something from the Pharmacy. When I came out of the store, there was a man with an accordion playing a patriotic song encouraging the people. How can that be. We are suppose to be down on our backs, but we seem to be encouraged through the storm.

Even praise unto God confuses the enemy. The Word says in Psalms 150:

(Psa 150:1 KJV) Praise ye the LORD. Praise God in his sanctuary: praise him in the firmament of his power.

(Psa 150:2 KJV) Praise him for his mighty acts: praise him according to his excellent greatness.

(Psa 150:3 KJV) Praise him with the sound of the trumpet: praise him with the psaltery and harp.

(Psa 150:4 KJV) Praise him with the timbrel and dance: praise him with stringed instruments and organs.

(Psa 150:5 KJV) Praise him upon the loud cymbals: praise him upon the high sounding cymbals.

(Psa 150:6 KJV) Let every thing that hath breath praise the LORD. Praise ye the LORD!"

In heaven, the angels are giving God continuous praise! Is there is anybody reading this book who is not ashamed to open their mouth and give God glory and praise. Psa 134:1-2 says, "Behold, bless ye the LORD, all ye servants of the LORD, which by night stand in the house of the LORD. Lift up your hands in the sanctuary, and bless the LORD.

America, let's keep confusing the enemy. We are coming out of this war with our hands up praising the Lord....through the storm and through the rain. America, as long as we keep our hands in the hand of the Master, we will win this war and have peace.

I want to do like those four beast around the throne of God. The Bible says that they cry "Holy," continuously. They give thanks unto God, continuously. Day and night they cry,

122.

"Holy; and we have learned from the 9th verse of Chapter 4 that 'holy' is a way of giving God thanks.

I wondered why they cry, "Holy," and the late Dr. E. V. Hill helped me with that. He said, "The reason why they bow and cry, "Holy," and then get back up; and then bow again, is because every time they bow, before they can get back up, the Lord has already done something else for them.

Somebody bowed this morning, got on your knees and cried thank you Lord, and before you could get back up, God had already done something else for you. If you understand what I am talking about, I can close this chapter. Why don't you give God some continuous praise:

If you praise Him, He'll lift your heavy burdens.
If you praise Him, He'll lighten your heavy load.
If you praise Him, He'll fix things for you.
If you praise Him, He'll heal your sick body.
If you praise Him, He'll bring you out alright.
If you praise Him, He'll wipe your weeping eyes
If you praise Him, He'll lift you up when you are falling down
If you praise Him, He'll help you through your storms

And you've got a right to praise Him.

Not only can we learn from these beast teach that 1. God is relevant for today, 2. God is almighty, 3 continuous praise is prerequisite for heaven, but 4, these four beast teach us that:

4. We should always give glory, honor and thanks unto Him. God has done so much for America, we should humble ourselves and open our mouths and openly give God praise!!!!!!! We should not worry about:

Who is watching us.
What we have on.
What education we don't have.
What people might say.
What the press might say....we night be surprised.
What the Evening News might say...we might be surprised.
Being embarrassed.
Our past mistakes.

123.

Our past due bills.
What other countries might say.....we might be pleasantly surprised

CHAPTER XXVI
GLORIFYING GOD

Excuse me please, but with all of the people dieing during this pandemic, I realize that I need to take a 'Praise Break' and give praise to our Lord. Please allow me in giving God thanks. Lord, you are so mighty, so gracious, so kind, so true, so ultra awesome, the most brilliant, so resplendent, so tremendous, so unusual, so uncommon, so incomparable, so fantastic, so beautiful, so incommensurable (nobody is equal to him), so exceeding, so divine, so noteworthy, so remarkable, so renowned, so extraordinary, so illustrious, so glorious, so marvelous, so wonderful, so wondrous, so amazing, so astounding, so enormous, so prodigious, the biggest of the big, the largest of the huge, so faithful, kind and true, from everlasting to everlasting thou art God, so ultra phenomenal, so great, my love, my joy, my hope and my peace. Thank you Lord for everything you have done for me! Amen.

CHAPTER XXVII
SHAKE OFF THE BEAST
(Acts 28 1-5)

This Coronavirus and pandemic is a Beast.......hundreds of thousand are infected with it and thousands of people have died. It is spreading so rampant that it is difficult to keep up with the numbers. the numbers are changing every hour. It's a Beast. However, we can shake off the Beast. Let me give you one example of someone who shook off the beast and then I will close this chapter. It is found in Acts 28:4 .

The Principle Person: The Apostle Paul
The Minor Persons: The mariners who were on the ship with Paul
The Time Line: This happened around A.D. 63....in other words around 63 years after the death of Jesus Christ.
The Location: The Island called Melita near Crete as they were taking Paul to Caesar in Rome
The Historicity: Reflects that the Jews accused Paul of preaching heresies among tem...that God could raise the dead; but Paul petitioned unto Caesar in Rome; and as they sailed the sea to Rome on the Mediterranean taking Paul to Caesar in Rome to plead his case before Caesar, a tempestuous wind came and began to break up the ship. They all had to swim to shore, but all the mariners were saved (246 in all). When they reached the shore, it was raining and cold, and as Paul gathered a few sticks and started a fire, a viper attached itself to the hand of Paul. The soldiers kept watching Paul expecting Paul to swell up and die, but Paul simply shook off the
beast into the fire, and instead, the beast died.

America has a beast (a serpent) attacking it and so far, we have not been able to shake it off into the fire. Why? We are not facing the real problem. The essence of the problem is not simply a health problem, or a scientific problem, this is a spiritual problem; and how can we solve a problem unless we face it.

The God of this earth (Jehovah God) is angry because we (his people) have forgotten Him and gone a whoring after other gods. It is a shame. We have tried to make everything else a god and disrespected the only true and living God...our creator....the creator of the ends of the earth. Who wouldn't be angry if people treated you that way after you had done so much for them. The President even wants the governors of the states in America to be appreciative for what he has done for them. How much more should God expect the world that He created to be appreciative for what HE has done for them? I would be angry too.

We have made gods out of sports figures and GOD gave them the strength to do what they do. It's alright to appreciate people. That's not what I am saying; but when we have made gods out of talented singers and Holly Wood stars, and GOD is the one who gave them the talent to do what they do, but we forget about him (that's wrong!). Every one has received credit except the one that the credit belongs to.....GOD Jehovah. Exodus 20:3 (KJV) God said, "Thou shalt have no other gods before me." Now we are trying to give all the creditt for any good results concerning the Coronavirus to the doctors....and we are grateful for any good advise they have given to the American people; however they are really not the ones that deserve the credit. They wouldn't even be able to think if GOD had not created brain cells.

How can we shake off the beast, if there is no fire; and we cannot build a fire throughout America until we start recognizing GOD, the creator of it all; but I believe, <u>with GOD'S help</u>, We will shake off this beast into the fire and it will shrivel up and die. Amen, and Amen.

CHAPTER XXVIII
SHOUT IN YOUR LIVING ROOM

When COVID 19 (this Coronavirus) is over...and it will be over, that's what people all over the world should do. We don't even need to wait til the battle is over. By faith we ought to start shouting NOW! Why? Faith moves God. Hebrews 11:6 (KJV) tells us, "But without faith it is impossible to please him: for he that cometh to God must believe that he is, and that he is a rewarder of them that diligently seek him." Hebrews 11:1 (KJV) proclaims, "Now faith is the substance of things hoped for, the evidence of things not seen." In America, we are only at the hope stage, but I believe that we will defeat this unseen COVID 19, and when we do, we will have the evidence of things not seen.

126.

In Matthew 17:20 (KJV), "Jesus said unto them (His disciples)...for verily I say unto you, If ye have faith as a grain of mustard seed, ye shall say unto this mountain, Remove hence to yonder place; and it shall remove; and nothing shall be impossible unto you."

I believe in what the Lord said, and if you believe it too, get out your shouting shoes and plan to shout in your living room. According to Philippians 4:13, we can do all things through Christ which strengthens us......and in 1 John 4:4b (KJV) it tells us that...... ". . . greater is he that is in you (us in America and all over the world), than he that is in the world (the enemy). Last but not the least, Jesus said in John 16:33b (get ready to shout in your living room),, "In the world ye shall have tribulation: but be of good cheer; I have overcome the world." Shout! Shout!! Shout!!! Shout!!!! Shout!!!!! We have the victory!

CHAPTER XXVIX
YOU DO IT FIRST

The purpose of this chapter is to help defeat the enemy....I have discovered a unique way of defeating the enemy when he brings detrimental things. You see, the enemy is working diurnally (daily) to defeat God's people, but I want you to know that if you resist the enemy, James 4:7 tells us that he will flee from us. When we perspicaciouly examine Rev. 12:9 and Rev. 20:1-3 we see that the enemy is continuously losing his power. So why do we continuously fear the enemy....and when we look at his ending of the Word of God in Rev. 20:10, we are assured that there is no need to fear the enemy.

Please allow me to give you just one testimony about 'You Do It First', and then I will close this chapter.

127.

Testimony...........My brother, (the brother right under me, Michael Johnson) went to Viet Nam and fought in the war. When he returned from Nam, he got hooked on drugs to help him cope with the aftermath. He became very depressed, in fact so depressed that he was considering suicide. One day when he was all alone sitting in his car, he heard a voice in his mind say, "Michael, you have been wanting to kill yourself, I tell you what you should do. You see that tree way down there at the end of the block? Mash on you accelerator as hard as you can and hold it down as you run into that tree going as fast as you can. You will instantly end it. Guess what my brother Michael told the enemy???? "YOU DO IT FIRST!!!!! (LOL)

Mr. President, this pandemic is all over the world, and many people will be trying various things to help, but may I suggest when it comes to humbling yourself in prayer, seeking God's face, and suggesting to everyone to turn from their wicked ways, YOU DO IT FIRST. One of these old days, some National Leader in the eye of the media is going to get the idea of leading the world in prayer. Mr. President, with all due respect, you are the leader of the most powerful nation in the world. May I suggest to you........... "YOU DO IT FIRST." It will touch the hearts of the people all over the world and change the destiny of the world.

CHAPTER XXX
SING IN THE MIDST OF YOUR STORM

While you read this book, think of an uplifting song, because I want you singing in your mind. Even if you say you are not a singer, I want to say that again....."I want you singing while you read the final pages of this book." I know some of you may not understand why, but help me to explain it a little bit by saying this proclamation:

During this pandemic, I saw on the news people in Italy singing out of the windows in their apartment buildings. It inspired me. I said to myself, "that's the way to do it." It reminded me of the movie "The Titanic". While the ship was going down, the people were singing and the musicians were playing.

128.

I don't believe that America is going down, but singing can bring joy to the soul and peace to the mind. Whenever you are going through a storm, learn to sing in the midst of your storm. It will be therapy to your soul and cause healing inside your heart.

My singing is a little different. I am a saxophone player, so whenever I get really down, I get my saxophone and began to sing on it. My saxophone is my voice. I have been told by many people, "When you play your saxophone, it sounds like you are singing." They didn't know that is exactly what I am doing......singing through my saxophone.

I have a grandson who is so funny (Raphael Rhone, Jr.) Whenever he becomes afraid, he begins to sing, and the more afraid he becomes, the louder he gets (LOL). One day he was in the bath-room, and you could here him singing all over the house. I knew he must have been a little afraid. You don't have to do like my grandson....sing when you are afraid, but may I suggest to you, 'learn to sing in the midst of your storms. It will make things a little easier for you and help calm your nerves. "Sing!!!"

1. If you are sick in the hospital. Sing!!!
2. When your bills are do. Sing!!!
3. When people lie on you. Sing!!!
4. When you have been cheated. Sing!!!
5. When people talk about you. Sing!!!
6. When your money is low. Sing!!!
7. When you are dissapointed. Sing!!!
8. When you are frustrated. Sing!!!
9. When you are depressed. Sing!!!
10. When you have sorrow. Sing!!!
11. When you are up. Sing!!!
12. When you are down. Sing!!!
13. During the COVID 19. Sing!!!
14. When your nerves are bad. Sing!!!
15. When you have stress. Sing!!!
16. When all hope seems to be gone. Sing!!!
17. When you have been bruised. Sing!!!
18. When you have been wounded. Sing!!!
19. When your path is dark. Sing!!!
20. When your way gets dim. Sing!!!
21. In the morning. Sing!!!
22. In the evening. Sing!!!
23. When the sun goes down. Sing!!!

24. Through the storms. Sing!!!
25. Through the rain. Sing!!!
26. Through the good times. Sing!!!
27. Through the bad times. Sing!!!
28. When nobody believe in you. Sing!!!
29. When people call you crazy. Sing!!!
30. When no one will listen to you. Sing!!!
31. In the midnight hour. Sing!!!
32. When you are hurting so badly. Sing!!!
33. When your bills are due. Sing!!!
34. When you are on lock-down. Sing!!!
35. When you are being quarantined. Sing!!!
36. When it looks like there is no hope. Sing!!!
37. If this pandemic separate you from your family. Sing!!!
38. If it looks like this Coronavirus is over. Sing!!!

I know you are hurting, and I know you are going through; but may I give you some good advise? When you are going through your storms, just start singing. Get your radio, your music box and some head phones, shut the world out, and start singing.

Example....one of our Ambassadors was the late Bishop Gary Stern in North Chicago. He had a very prestigious job and the Managers around him were jealous of him....and they plotted against him and decided that they would try to degrade him. So they ordered him to go out to the parking lot and sweep the parking lot. They just knew they

would break him.....that he would get mad and quit. But Pastor Stern put his gospel music on and put ear phones in his ears and started singing with the gospel music. When the bosses saw that he could handle any kind of situation, they promoted him to manager.

I've come to tell you to learn to sing in the midst of your storms. Please allow me to give you a few more examples of people who have sang through their storms:

1. My brother David drives one of those huge ¾ ton trucks. A lady was backing out of her drive way not watching and hit his truck. It severely damaged his back. He wasn't able to work for months. He still can't work without sever back pains. But David started singing through prayer, and GOD heard his song. Incredible things started to happening for him. He

2. sang so loud through prayer that God gave me a dream about him. The next Sunday morning, immediately after my church service, I got my deacons and went over to his church (he is a Pastor also) and I presented him an offering for a little over $500. After that I said, "I better learn how to sing. (LOL)
3. Moses: when GOD saved Moses and the Children of Israel from Pharoah and his army while crossing the Red Sea, the Bible says after this happened, the Bible said in Exodus 15:1, "Moses began to sing. Then sang Moses and the children of Israel this song unto the LORD, and spake, saying, I will sing unto the LORD, for he hath triumphed gloriously: the horse and his rider hath he thrown into the sea." Verse 12 says, "The LORD is my strength and song, and he is become my salvation: he is my God, and I will prepare him an habitation; my father's God, and I will exalt him.
4. When the children of Israel were in the wilderness and needed water, and God gave them water from the stream that led to Ar, by the border of Moab....and the princes and nobles dug a well for the people...in (Num 21:17 KJV) Israel sang this song, "Spring up, O well; sing ye unto it:"
5. 1 Sam 21:11 tells us that the servants of Achish said unto him, Is not this David the king of the land? did they not sing one to another of him in dances,
6. saying, Saul hath slain his thousands, and David his ten thousands?
7. 1 Sam 18:6 (KJV) tells us, when David returned from the slaughter of Goliath the Philistine, the women came out of the cities of Israel, singing and dancing, "Saul hath slain his thousands, but David ten thousands."
8. You do remember that God had given David so many victories that in (2 Sam 22:50 (KJV) David sang praises unto thy name.
9. Proverbs 29:6 tells us that "The righteous doth sing and rejoice.
10. Isaiah 12:5 says, "Sing unto the LORD; for he hath done excellent things."
11. Paul said in Heb 2:12 "...in the midst of the church will I sing praise unto thee, O Lord."
12. James 5:13 tells us, "Is any among you afflicted? let him pray. Is any merry? let him sing psalms."
13. And then in the end, Rev 15:1 tells us that seven angels having the seven last plagues will stand on a sea of glass with the harps of God and sing this song......"Great and marvellous are thy works, Lord God Almighty; just and true are thy ways, thou King of saints."

Listen, you may not be able to carry a tune, but you better learn to sing in the midst of your storms. It will bring you great comfort. I heard a funny story: a man fell in love

131.

with this woman <u>because she could sing real, real good</u>; but she was ugly as a bull dog. And he married her. On their wedding night, when it was time to have intimacy, she took off her eye lashes, and he didn't have a problem with that......then her wig.....he still didn't have a problem with that .....then she took out her teeth, he still didn't have a problem with that; but then she removed her leg....(now remember he married her just because she could sing real good). When she removed her leg, guess what he said......"BABY YOU BETTER START SINGING!!!!!!!!!!!! (LOL)

Listen singing can help you feel:
1. Joy
2. Peace
3. Hope
4. Resolve
5. Comfort
6. Gratification
7. A calm
8. Love
9. Feel protected
10. Less frustrated
11. Less tense
12. Less stressful
13. Less fear
14. Feel comfort
15. Less sick
16. Less afflicted
17. Victorious
18. Prosperous
19. Triumphant
20. BLESSED!!!

Singing in the midst of a storm can make things better. If you are facing COVID 19 and this pandemic may I suggest that you learn how to sing through your storms.

CHAPTER XXXI
IS THERE ANY THING TOO HARD FOR GOD?

May I give you my answer? NO!!!!!!!!!!!! There is nothing too hard for God. If that is your answer too, why don't you turn that faith in God toward the Coronavirus. There is nothing too hard for God. John 1:3 tells us that God made everything, including the Coronavirus; and I want to reiterate this again......I'm glad God made the Coronavirus (God made both good and evil for His glory) Why? Why am I glad that GOD made the Coronavirus???? Because if GOD had not made the Coronavirus, the enemy (the devil) would have tried to make it just so he could become as GOD; and if the enemy had made it....you think it's bad right now??? If Satan had made the Coronavirus, he would have killed not only over forty thousand people worldwide, he would have killed every person on the face of this earth who is trying to do something good......Christians. Satan is like a jealous fien. He says "If I can't have you, nobody can." So thank GOD, that He made the Coronavirus. If we humble ourselves and pray, seek God's face and turn from our wicked ways, I believe God would order the Coronavirus to leave this world. There is NOTHING too hard for GOD!!!!

Abraham believed God. He believed that there is nothing too hard for God. When two angels came to his house he rushed and had a meal prepared for them and washed their feet. When they told his Wife Sarah that, at around this time next year, you shall have a child, Sarah laughed. However, Sarah was around 90 and Abraham was around 100 years of age, but they had a child around that time the next year. Wow!!!!!!! Is there ANYTHING to hard for God????? From what happened to Abraham and Sarah I learned some things and I want to share them with you who are reading this book. Here they are:

1. **Honor the Lord with your substance**......That is what Abraham did when the angels of God arrived at his house. Look at Genesis 18:5 (NIV) Let me get you something to eat, so you can be refreshed and then go on your way--now that you have come to your servant." "Very well,"they answered, "do as you say." Abraham got his servants to prepare some bread, some meat and he sat some milk before them while they prepared the tender cow that had been carefully selected.

2. **Let there be a sense of urgency about the Lord**. Gen 18:6 (NIV) tells us, "So Abraham hurried into the tent to Sarah. "Quick," he said, "get three seahs of fine flour and knead it and bake some bread." (Gen 18:7 NIV) Then he ran to the herd and selected a choice, tender calf and gave it to a servant, who hurried to prepare it."

3. **When God pronounces a blessing over you, don't laugh.** Have faith to believe what God said. Where did you find that Dr. Johnson? Look at Genesis 18:12 (NIV) When the angle of God told Sarah and Abraham that she would have a baby around that time the next year, it says, "So Sarah laughed to herself as she thought, "After I am worn out and my master is old, will I now have this pleasure?" In Genesis 18:13 (NIV) it tells us, "Then the LORD said to Abraham, "Why did Sarah laugh and say, 'Will I really have a child, now that I am old?'"

4. **Is there any thing too hard for the Lord?** It happened! Sarah had a baby around that time the next year. Ha ha ha ha ha ha ha ha HA!!!!!! Genesis 18:14 (NIV) asked the question, "Is there anything too hard for the LORD?

   Now, I believe that we can apply this to our present situation. The angle of the Lord said, " I will return to you at the appointed time next year and Sarah will have a son." Notice how God speaks...."Sarah will"....not "Sarah might" God doesn't speak that way with a question mark. God knows what will happen. He knows what will happen America too.

   This is HUGE!!!! God didn't say "Sarah might....GOD said "Sarah WILL". Everything God says is a faith statement. He believes in Himself. 'You' have to believe in Him too. If God says, "Whatsoever you bind on earth shall be bound in heaven....believe Him!!!!

   God asked 'IS there anything', not 'might there be anything'. 'IS' is in the present tense.In other words, "now"....is there anything in your present situation.....right now!......too hard for God. Too hard for the Lord....is there anything in your present situation that God cannot fix? And if you don't laugh like Sarah did (and don't doubt, but instead believe God, you shall have whatsoever you say).

   Let me cross reference this just to make sure I am on it. In Matthew 21:21 (KJV). Jesus cursed a fig tree. When the disciples saw it again, they were so amazed that it had dried up after Jesus cursed the fig tree. But "Jesus answered and said unto them, Verily I say unto you, If ye have faith, and doubt not, ye shall not only do this which is done to the fig tree, (but you can do more) but also (in addition to this) if ye shall say unto this mountain, Be thou removed, and be thou cast into the sea; it shall be done.

Then a little later in the same chapter, when the disciple could not cast the demons out of the lunatic boy (Matthew 1714-17 (KJV) shows us what happens when people don't believe God. "And Jesus said unto them (His disciples who asked why they could not cast the demonn out

134.

of the lunatic boy), Because of your unbelief: for verily I say unto you, If ye have faith as a grain of mustard seed, ye shall say unto this mountain, Remove hence to yonder place; and it shall remove; and nothing shall be impossible unto you." Even Jesus says there is NOTHING too hard if you will move under the auspices of GOD.

Let us look at what God will do for you if you don't laugh....but instead, believe God. (Matthew 16:19 (KJV) proclaims "And I will give unto thee the keys of the kingdom of heaven: and whatsoever **thou shalt bind on earth shall be bound in heaven: and whatsoever thou shalt loose on earth shall be loosed in heaven.**

Let us look at some of the things that some people thought was too hard for God:

1. God healing cancer, asthma, COPD, Emphysema, back, leg & heart problems.
2. Setting us debt free
3. Totally renovating this building.
4. Putting an elevator in the building so that our seniors can have access to the building. How are they going to enjoy it if they can't see the improvements...not only in the sanctuary, but upstairs, downstairs and on every floor. We need that elevator so that these mothers can walk on these floors pleading the blood of Jesus.
5. Having a baby when the doctors say you can't
6. Receiving your inheritance
7. Finding a good paying job
8. Getting your husband or wife motivated

GOD has done all of the the things above. There is NOTHING too hard for God!!!!!!!!!

CHAPTER XXXII
BINDING & LOOSING

Matt:16:13-19

Again, I have come to help all of us get blessed, not just for some days, but for every day this year and even beyond. I'm tired of the enemy cutting, wounding and bruising the people of God. You do remember that the Word of God says in John 10:10 (KJV) "The thief cometh not, but for to steal, and to kill, and to destroy: I am come that they might have life, and that they might have it more abundantly."

135.;

I found this key to blessings in the Word of God in Matthew. It is right in our chapter Matthew 13-19; and I want everyone in this house to read this because if you apply this one principle to your life today, this will cause you to be blessed all year long and even in the future. Is there anyone reading this book who wants to be blessed all year long and even in the future....if so shout "Yes!!!" Again, it is found in Matt. 16:13-19. Let's look at it.

And if we cross reference these scriptures, we find that in (1 Sam 30:6 KJV), King David loosed blessings on himself.....While King David and his men were out fighting his enemies, some other enemies doubled back on him and burned his home (Ziklag) to the ground and took his family and his wives, and many of the people captive. They took all the spoil and burned Ziklag to the ground. And David was greatly distressed; for the people spake of stoning him, because the soul of all the people were grieved, every man for his sons and for his daughters: but <u>David encouraged himself</u> in the LORD his God.

Let's go back to our chapter in Matthew 16:18-19 (KJV) which says, "And I say also unto thee, That thou art Peter, and upon this rock I will build my church; and the gates of hell shall not prevail against it.

Verse 19, "And I will give unto thee the keys of the kingdom of heaven: and whatsoever thou shalt bind on earth shall be bound in heaven: and whatsoever thou shalt loose on earth shall be loosed in heaven." God gave Peter the power to bind things on earth and even to lose them. How? Who?? How!!!

1. The keys of the kingdom of heaven..........now to find out how Peter received the keys to the kingdom of heaven, let us look at Peter. He was not a perfect man. He would lie and even cut you if he was pushed too far; but God gave him the keys to the kingdom of heaven....and heaven is the place where the stars of heaven are blessed not just one day, but every day. What was special about Peter??? Peter is the only one who said, "Thou art the Christ, the Son of the living God." He got it! In other words, Peter was the only one who exemplified great faith in Jesus. He wasn't just along for the ride. He was listening at every word that Jesus said, and what is better than that.....he believed every word that Jesus said.

   Faith moves God and God's son is just like Him. Faith moved Jesus. Most people on the earth at that time including the disciples couldn't believe that Jesus was truly the son of God, but Peter did. Therefore, because of Peter's faith in Jesus, Jesus decided to use Peter as an example; and he gave him the Keys to the kingdom of heaven. He gave him the power to bind and lose on earth, and whatever he bound on earth, God promised Peter that He would bind in heaven. Wow!!!!!!!! What a privilege.....so much power.

136.

Peter was in 'that' dispensation and time, but 'we'.....the saints of God are right now....in this dispensation time, and the baton has been passed to us. 'We' believe that JESUS is the Christ, the Son of the living God; and now, we have the privilege and the power to bind things and to lose things on this earth; and whatever we bind on this earth shall be bound in heaven, and whatever we lose on earth shall be loosed in heaven. Hallelujah!!!!!!!!!!

How do we bind and lose things on this earth??? We speak to it. Let's take time to bind some things........................We bind:

1. COVID 19........we bind:
2. Sicknesses
3. Disease
4. Lack
5. Poverty
6. Jealousy
7. Un-forgiveness
8. Unbelief
9. Disappointment
10. Frustrations
11. Everything that's not like the Lord
12. Confusion
13. Anger
14. Things that hold me back
15. Hatred
16. Destruction of my family
17. Curses on me and my family
18. Generational curses on me and my family
19. Depressions
20. Pain
21. Being bruised
22. Being wounded
23. Frustrations
24. Stress
25. Defeat
26. Lust
27. Lies told on me and my family
28. Evil against me and my family
29. Unforgiveness in my heart
30. Unrighteousness in me and my family

Chief Ambassador Dr. Vernard Johnson   **GOD'S CURE TO THE CORONAVIRUS**

31. IRS problems
32. Family problems
33. Police trouble on me and my family
34. Prison trouble on me and my family
35. Conniving spirits
36. Demons
37. Demonic plans against me & my family
38. My family from being sifted like wheat
39. Trouble with my eyes....ears....my talking, my walking
40. Being taken for granted
41. Being disrespected
42. Evil being done against me

Then the Bible says in Matthew 16:19, "Whatever you loose on earth......shall be loosed in heaven. We loose:

1. Great health
2. Great strength
3. No sicknesses
4. No lack
5. The blessings of the Lord to make me rich
6. The blessings of the Lord to make me wealthy
7. No poverty
8. I have a plenty
9. Our Inheritance
10. I am blessed
11. My family is blessed
12. We are loved
13. Every curse on me or my family is broken
14. Generational curses are broken.
15. No depression
16. No hatred toward me or my family
17. Joy in my soul
18. Peace in my mind
19. I am successful
20. I am more than a conqueror
21. I can do all things through Christ
22. I am triumphant
23. I am a winner

24. I am the head and not the tail
25. My territory is being enlarged
26. I have a great paying job
27. I am receiving promotions
28. I am receiving raises
29. I have favor everywhere
30. I have a new car
31. I am happy and not sad

CHAPTER XXXIII
FORGIVENESS

(Mark 11:25 KJV) And when ye stand praying, forgive, if ye have ought against any: that your Father also which is in heaven may forgive you your trespasses. (Mark 11:26 KJV) But if ye do not forgive, neither will your Father which is in heaven forgive your trespasses.

O people of GOD, we must learn to forgive. No matter what people have done to us, we must learn to forgive. People are like little children.....they are mean. They say mean things and they do mean things. Most of the time, they are not aware how much they are hurting someone. They seem to only realize pain when God allows it to come back to them. Then it helps them to grow up from childhood to an adult.

I am writing this book during a pandemic, and we have to be careful that we don't hurt people, especially the ones we love the most. Stress is all around us and many times stress will cause people to say, do, think, not show kindness, forget about, and not to show that you love someone when they really, really need you; but let us learn to forgive.

As you read this chapter, I want to talk about 'forgiveness'. My purpose is to cause all of us to think about some areas of forgiveness in a way that perhaps we have never considered. When you forgive, you let go of all negative emotions such as taking revenge on someone, and you wish the offender well. To forgive is to accept an apology....to get rid of a grudge, to completely let some hard feelings go, or to cease from being angry about something.

139.

The word forgiveness is made up of '3' different participles.....the preposition 'for', refers to '<u>on behalf of someone</u>', in favor of, or for the sake of someone else....in other words, to 'do it for someone else'.. When you hear the word 'for' it means that you are giving something on behalf of someone else. The forgiveness may not be for you....it may be for someone else. The second word 'give' means <u>to provide something</u>....to present or impart something to someone else. When you forgive, <u>you may be giving someone else some peace, some joy, some hope.</u> And you see, sometimes when you forgive, the forgiveness is not for the other person, the forgiveness is to help 'you' too

Please allow me to give you one of my testimonies. I had an Elder in one of our churches call me and ask if he could borrow $2,500..........He sounded pretty desperate. I must have had a tax refund or something on hand, so I loaned him the $2,500 that he said he needed. He told me that he would pay me back in a couple of weeks. Two weeks past and and he did not pay me back. A whole month passed and he did not pay me back. Two months, three months, six months passed and he did not pay me back; but every time I would see him, he would always say to me, "I'm gonna pay you, I'm gonna pay you." Even when I wasn't even thinking about him, if I looked at him he would say, "I'm gonna pay you!"

Finally, after around a year, the Lord spoke to my heart and said, "I want you to forgive that Elder of that loan you made to him for $2,500. At first, I thought it was the devil speaking to my heart, but I eventually knew without a doubt it was the Lord. So I called him, and before I could say anything, he blurted out, "I'm gonna pay you, I know I owe you that money and I'm gonna pay you!" I interrupted him and said, "Elder, I'm not calling you to get you to pay me, I'm calling to tell you that I forgive the loan that I made to you. He replied, "What!!!!!!" I said, "Yes, the Lord told me to forgive you of that loan." He thanked me several times, and then we hung up our phones.

Around two weeks later that Elder died. I was soooooooooooo happy that I followed the Lord. If I had not forgiven that man of that money, I probably 140.

would have felt that the pressure that he felt about owing me that money helped to kill him; but I felt free in my spirit and relieved. I had no guilt. Why, because I had forgiven him. The forgiveness was not only for him...it was to help me. To keep me from getting sick, from dying myself...God helps people to overcome through forgiveness

The 3rd participle in forgiveness is **'ness'**, and 'ness' is a suffix attached to adjectives and participles **giving them quality and a state of being**. The suffix helps to give these adjectives a state of being....such as being kind is a great attribute..but kindness is a state of being, goodness, and being righteous is a

140.

wonderful characteristic, but righteousness is a state of being.

1. Our daughter (Lynitra)—when she was around 7 years old, went to school and during 'show and tell' she told her Principle at her school that my wife and I eat snakes and spiders.....I was a little angry at her until I get her explanation. When I asked her why she told her Principle that she responded, "Dad, they were having 'Show &Tell' that day in my class, and I didn't have anything to 'Show & Tell'. So being the only Black in the classroom I didn't want to be embarrassed. So I made up something and told them (and I said it real proud like), "My Dad and Mom eat snakes and spiders!!!" Then she added, "And Dad that day I was the most popular little girl at school. Everyone wanted to talk to me and spend time with me. You would have thought I was a rock star." (LOL) Well, I had to forgive her, even though her Principle called me and asked if my wife and I ate snakes and spiders. I had to forgive.

May I share with you some famous people who had to learned to forgive?

Nelson Mandela—after being imprisoned for 20 years in South Africa.... he forgave. Mandela said "When you partially forgive "You heal part of the pain." But when you completely forgive, "You heal ll the pain."

God is the most forgiving person in the world today. You say, how can you say God is the most forgiving person in the world today.....God is God....
Well, if the Holy Ghost is the 3rd 'person' of the Trinity, what does that make Jesus and God? Since the Holy Ghost is the 3rd person and God and Jesus are all 3 in one....that's make Jesus the 2nd 'person' and God the 1st person. Again, GOD is and has been the most forgiving PERSON in the history of the world.

One of the greatest examples of forgiveness in the Word of God is the example that God gives concerning his bride....Israel...or as some people call them...the Israelites....and God through this exemplifies our chapter today found in Mark 11:26, "But if ye do not forgive, neither will your Father which is in heaven

141.

forgive your trespasses." God forgives these precious people (his bride..the Israelites) over and over and over and over and over and over and over and over and over and over again. I still didn't put enough overs in there. But it is quite evident that God forgave them, because now 'we' are the 'New Israelites' And from the forgiveness we see with God, that is why people say that we shouldn't ask God for 'one more chance'......we should ask God for 'another chance', because most of us reading this book have already used up 'another chance'. We have messed up over and over and over and over and over again.

Just wait til I remind you of just some of the times God has forgiven people:

1. In the beginning, when God created Adam and Eve.......
2. After God made man and Cain killed his brother Able....
3. In Exodus 20:12, God said to "Honor thy father and thy mother: that thy days may be long upon the land which the LORD thy God giveth thee." Man, many times doesn't do that. He honors everyone else and forgets all about God, but God forgives.
4. In Exo 20:13, God said, "Thou shalt not kill." and yet we kill with our tongues.
5. In Exo 20:14, Thou shalt not commit adultery, and yet man commits adultery....but God forgives.
6. In Exo 20:15, God said, "Thou shalt not steal....and yet man steals
7. In Exo 20:16, God said, "Thou shalt not bear false witness against thy neighbour," and yet man does the opposite", but God forgives.
8. In Exo 20:17, God said, "Thou shalt not covet thy neighbor's house, thou shalt not covet thy neighbor's wife, nor his manservant, nor his maidservant, nor his ox, nor his ass, nor any thing that is thy neighbor's.....and yet we do the opposite, yet God forgives.
9. After man had sinned so badly, God decided to destroy the entire world but one righteous man Noah. God must have forgiven because He started the world all over again.
10. The children of Israel making that idol God....and Moses throwing the 10 commandments down the mountainside. God was very angry, but he forgave.
11. When God accepted the blood of animals as a sacrifice because man had sinned so much.
12. When God needed a sacrifice for sin once and for all, and Jesus said he would go.
13. When God sent his son, and man treated His son so badly
    a. They sent him to judgement hall after judgment hall...and God forgave ..
    b. They whipped Jesus all night long....and God forgave them.
    c. They marched Him up to Calvary.....and God forgave them.
    d. They layed the Messiah on a old wooden cross....and God forgave them.
    e. They nailed His hands...yet God forgave them.
    f. They nailed His feet....yet God forgave them.

    g. The pierced Him in the side....yet God forgave them.
    h. He hung His head and gave up the ghost...and yet God forgave them.

Again, God is the most forgiving person ever in the history of the whole wide world.

We see Christ exemplified in our chapter: Mark 11:25 (KJV) "And when ye stand praying, forgive, if ye have ought against any: that your Father also which is in heaven may forgive you your trespasses." Mark 11:26 (KJV) says, "But if ye do not forgive, neither will your Father which is in heaven forgive your trespasses."

2. **I want to remind you about The GREEN RIVER KILLINGS. You might** remember seeing this on the news—Gary Leon Ridgway was better known as the infamous Green River Killer. In 2003, he confessed to the murders of 60 women...many of them prostitutes. At his trial in 2003, the court allowed the families of the victims to speak in front of him. What anger and grief they showed, but Ridgway showed no remorse until Robert Rule, the father of a 16 year old girl (Linda Jane Rule), came up and said <u>something unexpected</u>. Rule said these words, and I quote, **"Mr. Ridgeway....there are people here that hate you. I'm not one of them. You've made it difficult to live up to what I believe, and that is what God says to do,..... to forgive.......(then he paused and said) "Mr. Ridgeway, you are forgiven, Sir. Then he took his seat. A few seconds later, Mr. Ridgeway began to weep.** <u>These are the only words that brought Ridgway to tears.</u>

It is sooooo grievous to realize that some people cannot forgive someone because of the petty things they did to you:

1. Somebody lied on you.............forgive them.
2. Somebody tried to scandalize your name........forgive them.
3. Somebody took your man, or somebody took your woman......you can get another one....forgive them.
4. Somebody gossiped about you...it was a lie....forgive them.
5. Somebody stole that position from you on your job or in the Jurisdiction.....you will get a better one....forgive them.
6. Somebody on purpose dug a ditch for you, but 'they' fell in it....forgive them.
7. Somebody used you like a dish rag.....forgive them...it's coming back to them.
8. Somebody stole your money...........
9. Somebody mistook your kindness for weakness.........
10. Somebody traded your 'best friends...best friendship' in for another.............
11. Somebody cheated you out of that house...you will get a better one....forgive

143.

12. Somebody wouldn't pick you up...........God will fix that....forgive
13. Somebody didn't treat you right at church................
14. Somebody talked about you, but you were innocent...............
15. Somebody called you stupid................perhaps you did something stupid.........
16. Somebody called you the 'n' word...................
17. Somebody didn't treat you right..........
18. Somebody forgot your birthday..................
19. Somebody stabbed you in your back..............
20. Somebody cut your throat..................you got to forgive them.
21. Somebody hurt your child.......................
22. Somebody wounded and bruised you......................
23. Somebody misunderstood you...................
24. Somebody lied on you 'in court'.......................
25. Somebody cheated in the marriage.......................
26. Somebody didn't pay you back the money you loaned them....................
27. Somebody stole your blessing and gave it to someone else.............
28. Somebody has been so unry to you and they hurt you so bad.....but forgive.
29. Somebody talked to you so badly....but forgive.
30. Somebody tried to take your life............but forgive .
31. Somebody's son or daughter is a cross-dresser, a transvestite.....but forgive
32. You found out that somebody is a homosexual-a lesbian..........forgive
33. Someone hurt you in the church...............forgive!!!!!

You see, un-forgiveness is a silent killer. Harboring un-forgivness in your heart will kill....you....dead! Do you realize some of the side effects unforgivness causes??????

1. Stress
2. Depression
3. Frustration
4. Heart trouble
5. Trouble in your brain
6. It affects your arteries
7. It affects your liver
8. It affects your kidneys
9. It affects your stomach
10. It affects your skin color
11. It affects your feet
12. It affects your eyes
13. It affects your speech

GOD'S CURE TO THE CORONAVIRUS   **Chief Ambassador Dr. Vernard Johnson**

144.

14. It can cause strokes
15. It can cause cancer
16. It can cause numbness in your legs
17. It can cause high blood pressure
18. It can cause low blood pressure
19. It can cause sadness
20. It can cause distress
21. It can cause anger
22. It can cause you to miss money
23. It can cause you to not prosper
24. It can cause you not to be triumphant
25. It can cause you not to have the victory
26. It can cause you to miss that promotion
27. It can cause you to destroy your relationship
28. It can cause you to destroy your future
29. It can destroy that relationship between you and your best friend.

Listen, we must forgive, forgive, forgive, forgive, forgive!!!........I don't care what someone did to you, I want you to live! Forgive, forgive, forgive, forgive, forgive, forgive!!!!......

But you say, "You don't know what they did to me." That's right, 'I' don't know, but GOD knows. It doesn't matter what they did to 'you'......the chances are, 'you' did much worse to them....but you will live much longer if you forgive. If you will forgive.....I said, if you will forgive.

I know it looks like this pandemic will kill all of us, but if I am going to go, I don't know about you, but I don't want to face my maker with un-forgiveness in my heart. Some people just cannot bring themselves to say, "I'm sorry." 'You' have to be the one. We need to be like Job. Even though he didn't know of anything his children had done, he
still made a sacrifice for them; and even though you may not of anything you have done to someone, it is still good to ask them to forgive you. If you can forgive, or if you want to be forgiven, I want you to call some people TODAY and tell them something like this:

1. If I mistreated you in any way, I am so sorry.
2. Please forgive me....and count it to my head and not my heart.
3. In the name of Jesus, I want you to know that I love you in the Lord.
4. Again, if you feel I have mistreated you, if you will forgive me;
5. I promise, I'll do better.

145.

And most of all, we need to tell God that we are sorry for all of our sins. I know a world wide revival would break out and the Coronavirus would dry up, if we would repent. Repent! Repent!Repent!! Repent!!! Repent!!!! Repent!!!!! Repent!!!!!!! Repent!!!!!!! Repent!!!!!!!!!

HELPS

1. The Wisdom of GOD
2. The Holy Bible (King James Version)
3. The Zondervan NIV Study Bible
4. Apple 8 iphone
5. The Life & Experiences of Chief Ambassador, Dr. Vernard Johnson

www.ingramcontent.com/pod-product-compliance
Lightning Source LLC
LaVergne TN
LVHW091553060526
838200LV00036B/826